The Hiker's Guide
to **TEXAS**

Laurence Parent

FALCON PRESS

Helena, Montana

ACKNOWLEDGMENTS

The book is dedicated to my wife Patricia, who accompanied me when she could, but mostly patiently endured my long absences.

Several friends joined me for some of the hikes, Jo Lou Spleth in particular. Rick LoBello and Tom Alex at Big Bend, Larry Henderson at the Guadalupe Mountains, and Chuck Boettcher helped with suggestions and research. Several people at the Texas Parks and Wildlife Department helped with information and map research, including David Baxter, Jim Carrico, Marie LeMond, Tommy Powell, and June Secrist. Terri Eaton, Kent and Beth Brock, Candice Caperton, and Pat and Jay Caperton all offered me their hospitality during my travels. Governor Ann Richards, even with her busy schedule, was kind enough to write the introduction. My gratitude also goes to the many other people, such as Sara Kirkpatrick, who helped in ways big and small.

Special thanks go to Malcolm Bates, my editor, and the other people of Falcon Press who gave me the opportunity to present the best of the Texas outdoors.

Cover Photo:
South McKittrick Canyon in the Guadalupe Mountains
by Laurence Parent

CONTENTS

INTRODUCTION

THE HIKES

FOREWORD

Several years ago I heard a joke about a fellow from New York who was going to spend his vacation in Texas. "I don't have a lot of time," he said to a Texan friend of his, "and Texas is so big. I think I should just try to see one part of it. Which part do you recommend?"

His friend thought a moment, then replied, "The outside part."

Texas is a place of legendary bounty, and it has been richly blessed with natural beauty unlike any in the world. Our diversity is staggering. From the Big Bend region in far west Texas to the Gulf Coast, and from the fertile farmlands of the Rio Grande Valley to the flatlands and canyons of the Texas Panhandle, there is an infinite variety of landscape. An endless opportunity for people to enjoy the great outdoors!

This guidebook will serve a vital need, putting the variety of hiking opportunities in Texas into a form that is easy to reference. There is, in fact, so much in Texas to be explored that a person could be paralyzed by indecision. *The Hiker's Guide to Texas* lays out the choices, offers valuable suggestions, and provides the reader all the information she or he needs to plan a great and successful hiking adventure anywhere in the Lone Star State. Whether you will be hiking the mountains, islands, or forests, or exploring the Texas Hill Country or the Big Thicket, or even just strolling the many paths and parks in our great cities, this book will be a valuable resource.

One walk I heartily recommend is the path around Town Lake in Austin. The planners of the lake and the trails around it understood perfectly the special character that water can give a city. The view of Austin and the Texas Capitol over Town Lake is one of my favorites in the state, beautiful and inspiring. The trails are wide and clean, and on any one of Austin's typical clear summer days, they bustle with the vitality of Austin's colorful residents (and their dogs). Taking a long walk on these trails is one of my favorite ways to spend a Saturday morning.

I hope you will find as much pleasure in exploring the Texas outdoors as I have. And if you have any questions along the way, ask anyone. There isn't a Texan alive who doesn't love to talk about this special place.

Sincerely

Ann W. Richards,
Governor

LOCATION OF HIKES

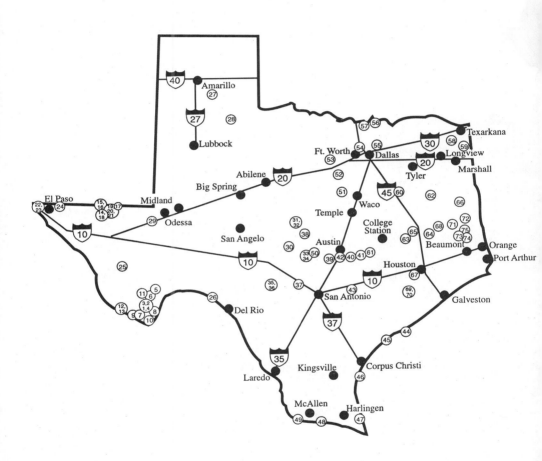

A world of hiking opportunities await hikers in Texas. Cave at the mouth of Rancherías Canyon

HIKING IN TEXAS, AN INTRODUCTION

Texas forms an enormous bridge between east and west, from the deep south on the Louisiana border to the old west in El Paso. Follow Interstate 10 for the 855 miles from El Paso to Orange, and you pass from the arid mountains and basins of the Chihuahuan Desert to the lush, fetid bayous of the Big Thicket. The change from north to south is no less extreme. On a given winter day, residents of Brownsville may be sweating in the citrus groves of the Rio Grande Valley while Amarillo shivers under two-foot drifts of snow.

People unfamiliar with the state often believe that Texas is little more than flat desert, grazed by underfed cows and littered with oil wells. However, Texas's tremendous size and wide elevation range creates a surprising variety of climates, vegetation, and terrain. East Texas receives fifty or more inches of rain annually and is covered with a mosaic of lakes and rivers. Bald cypresses and water tupelos line the swampy bayous, while dense pine forests blanket the uplands. Spanish moss festoons the live oaks, while fragrant magnolia blossoms perfume the air.

A visit to West Texas will convince skeptics that Texas is far from flat. Texas may not have the high elevations common in the western states, but the highest point, Guadalupe Peak, still reaches a respectable 8,749 feet. Its steep slopes and sheer cliffs tower a vertical mile above the salt flats at its base. Numerous other mountain ranges pepper West Texas, with many peaks reaching 7,000 or 8,000 feet.

Live oaks and junipers cloak the rolling terrain of the Hill Country, in the center of the state. Crystal-clear streams tumble down canyons cut through the limestone plateau. Secret places lie hidden in the folds of the hills: the fiery red maples of the deep canyons of the Sabinal River, the labyrinthine Caverns of Sonora, the pink granite dome of Enchanted Rock.

The Panhandle also guards its secrets. The Canadian River breaks the endless flat plain into a series of slopes and gullies. The Prairie Dog Town Fork of the Red River cuts an 800-foot deep gash known as Palo Duro Canyon. Gnarled junipers cling to the red and ocher slopes of the canyon. Hidden side canyons and eroded pinnacles belie the stark treeless plains above.

Elevation, the presence of the Gulf of Mexico, and the sheer size of the state largely control climate in Texas. The gulf provides a moisture source and moderating influence on the coastal areas of the state. Overall, Texas is a warm state because of its low latitude and low elevations. However, the Panhandle, because of its far northern reach, and the mountains of West Texas get at least a few short-lived snows every winter.

The state is noted for the diversity of its weather. No mountains block the flow of cold fronts from Canada in winter, so occasional northers interrupt the warm weather and bring surprising cold spells even in the southern part of the state. The northers sweep in suddenly, dropping temperatures thirty or forty degrees overnight. Historical temperature extremes in Texas run an incredible range, from -23 degrees to 120 degrees Fahrenheit.

A winter storm shrouds the Chisos Mountains.

In spring, cold fronts collide with warm moist gulf air and create tornadoes and severe thunderstorms. Fall can bring hurricanes to the coast. The September, 1900 hurricane that hit Galveston claimed over 6,000 lives, making it the worst natural disaster in American history. Fortunately, Texas weather is rarely extreme enough to hinder outdoor activities. All of the hikes in this guide can be done year round, although some seasons will be more pleasant than others. Except for West Texas, most of the state is fairly heavily populated and developed. Because of Texas's status as an independent republic before it joined the United States, little land remains in public hands. Thus, the only area of the state with large areas of accessible wilderness lie in West Texas. Because of their large size, Big Bend and Guadalupe Mountains National Parks are the premier wild areas of the state open to the public. However, Texas has been rapidly adding new state parks, many with beautiful scenery and hiking trails.

Quite a few of this guidebook's hikes are within the two national parks, but the majority are scattered across all parts of the state. I've included popular hikes, such as the South Rim at Big Bend, but also many obscure hikes, such as Matagorda Island. All of the hikes lie on public land, chiefly the state parks, national forests, and national parks. The vast majority of trailheads are accessible by any type of vehicle; only a few require high clearance or four-wheel drive. If you are a beginning hiker, don't let the length of some of these hikes intimidate you. Don't restrict yourself to only the short ones. Most of the long hikes are beautiful and rewarding even if you only go a half mile down the trail. Although the trails in this guide may keep you busy for years, many of the hike descriptions suggest additional nearby routes or extensions of the described hike. Don't be afraid to try them. This book serves best as an introduction to many of the most beautiful backcountry areas of Texas.

Using the Guide

The Hiker's Guide to Texas describes seventy-five hikes scattered widely across the state of Texas. The map at the start of this book indicates their locations. Several categories of information describe each hike. The general description gives a brief one-sentence description of the hike, along with its degree of difficulty. The general location gives the hike's location in relation to the closest significant town or park. The length gives the approximate length of the hike as a round trip; that is, the distance from the trailhead to the destination and back to the trailhead. The elevation lists the highest and lowest points reached on the hike. The maps category suggests maps to use for the hike. The best season gives the best time of year, weatherwise, for the hike. Water availability lists sites on the hike where water can be found. Special attractions describe some of the high points of the hike. Permit information is listed if permits are required to enter or camp in an area. Finding the trailhead provides detailed directions for locating the start of each hike. The hike provides a detailed description of the hike itself, usually with some introductory information about the area. Detailed maps accompany each hike. The map information was taken from USGS topo maps, national forest maps, state park maps, and national park maps. Use the guidebook's maps in conjunction with the government maps.

General description

The general description provides three categories of information. Besides giving a very brief summary of the hike, it assigns the hike its degree of difficulty and suggests the amount of time required for the hike. Assessing a hike's difficulty is very subjective. Not only do the elevation, elevation change, and length play a role, but trail condition, weather, and physical condition of the hiker are important. However, even my subjective ratings will give some idea of difficulty. To me, elevation gain was the most significant variable in establishing levels of difficulty. Most of the hikes, except in West Texas, have only small elevation gains and are rated easy or moderate. The majority of the difficult hikes are located in West Texas. In general, if a hike gains less than 1,000 feet and is less than eight miles round trip, I usually rated it as easy. Within each category there are many degrees of difficulty, of course. Obviously a two-mile hike gaining two hundred feet is going to be much easier than an eight-mile hike gaining 900 feet. Moderate hikes usually gain somewhere between 1,000 and 2,000 feet and run longer than eight miles. The strenuous hikes usually gain over 2,000 feet and are fairly long. Poor trails, excessive heat, high elevations with thin air, cross-country travel, and other factors may result in a more difficult designation than would otherwise seem to be the case from simply the elevation change and trail length. Carrying a heavy backpack can make even an "easy" day hike fairly strenuous.

The hiking speed of different people varies considerably. A hike is loosely classed as a day hike if most reasonably fit people can easily complete it in one day or less. Likewise, two- or three-day hikes can be easily done by most reasonably fit people in two or three days. Many of the day hikes, although easily done in one day, have attractions that make them worthy of longer, relaxed stays. A few of the day hikes, particularly in some of the National Park Service areas, must be done in a day because overnight camping is not allowed.

Length

The length specified in each description is listed as a round trip distance from the trailhead to the end of the route and back. As mentioned in the individual hike descriptions, some of the hikes work well with car shuttles. Setting up such shuttles with two cars can halve the round trip mileage of some of the walks. Alternatively, someone can pick up your group at a set time at the end of the route. Another method involves splitting the group, dropping off the first half at one end, and parking the car and starting the other half from the other end of the hike. When the two groups meet in the middle, they exchange car keys, allowing the first group to later pick up the second. All hike mileages assume, however, that you are unable to arrange a shuttle.

Hike lengths have been estimated as closely as possible using topographic maps and government measurements. However, the different sources do not always agree, so the final figure is sometimes the author's best estimate of the actual distance.

Elevation

Elevation is generally the most important factor in determining a hike's difficulty. The two numbers listed are the highest and lowest points reached on the hike. Often, but not always, the trailhead lies at the low point and the end lies at the highest point. With canyon hikes, the numbers are sometimes reversed. Many of the hikes in West Texas have a fairly steady climb going out and a fairly steady downhill coming back. Some of the hikes have several ups and downs on the way, requiring more elevation gain and effort than the high and low numbers indicate. The hikes along the coast and in South and East Texas generally have very minimal elevation changes. Absolute elevation also affects difficulty. At high elevations, lower atmospheric pressure creates "thin air." The thin air requires higher breathing rates and more effort to pull enough oxygen into the lungs. Since most of Texas lies at low elevations, hikers will encounter thin air on only a few of the hikes. The moderately high elevations encountered on hikes in the Chisos, Franklin, Davis, and particularly the Guadalupe Mountains will require only a little additional effort. Physically fit hikers coming from low elevation areas should acclimate easily within two or three days.

MAP LEGEND

Arrow		Described Trail & Trailhead	
Interstate		Alternate Trail and Trailhead	
U.S. Highway		Cross-Country Route	
State or Other Principal Road		Campsite/ Trailhead	
Forest Road	0000	Wilderness Boundary	
Dirt Road	= = =	State Boundary	
Paved Road		River, Creek, Drainage	
Improved Dirt Road		Bridge	
Mine or Tunnel		Spring	
Peak & Elevation	X 0000	Building	
Lakes		Locked Gate	
Cliffs			
Pass or Saddle			
Marsh or Meadow			

0   .5   1

Scale

Maps

The maps in this guide are as accurate and current as possible. When used in conjunction with the description and the maps listed in each hike's heading, you should have little trouble following the route. Generally, two types of maps are listed. Most of the state parks have excellent park and hiking maps available free at the entrance station or headquarters. The National Forest maps usually show the trails but, because of their small scale, rarely give enough detail to be especially helpful. However, they are very useful for locating forest roads, trailheads, and campgrounds. They are generally more current than the USGS topographic maps and usually show the level of improvement of the forest roads. Most of the National Park Service areas have maps or brochures showing the trails. Big Bend and the Guadalupe Mountains have excellent custom maps of the parks. USGS topographic quadrangles are generally the most detailed and accurate maps available of natural features. With some practice they allow you to visualize peaks, canyons, cliffs, rivers, roads, and many other features. With a little experience, a topographic map, and a compass, you should never become lost. They are particularly useful for little-used trails and off-trail travel. Unfortunately, many of the quadrangles, particularly in less-populated parts of the state, are out of date and do not show many newer manmade features such as roads and trails. However, they are still useful for their topographic information. The park and forest maps are usually available at park headquarters and at many outdoor shops in the larger cities.

USGS quads can usually be found at the same outdoor shops or ordered directly from USGS. To order, list the state, the number desired of each map, the exact map name as listed in the hike heading, and the scale. Send your order to the U.S. Geological Survey, ESIC-Denver, 169 Federal Building, 1961 Stout Street, Denver, CO 80294, (303) 844-4169. Call before sending your order to determine current prices.

Best season

The season specified for a hike is the optimum or ideal season. Since snow does not stay on the ground for extended periods of time in Texas, all of the trails in this guide can be hiked any time of year. However, since the state is usually hot in summer, the other three seasons generally provide the best weather for hiking. To escape the heat in summer, go to the West Texas mountains, or pick a hike with a good swimming hole. Spring is the rainy season in Central and East Texas but is still an excellent time to hike, with pleasant temperatures and fields of wildflowers. The rains fall in West Texas from July through September, but are short-lived and bring cooler temperatures. A few snows usually fall every year in the mountains and Panhandle, but they usually melt off within a day or two. Spring can be dry and windy in West Texas, making desert hikes unpleasant at times. Fall is probably the premier time for hiking anywhere in the state. Always check weather forecasts before starting your hike.

Water availability

Sources of water are listed if they are known to usually be reliable. Any water obtained on a hike should be purified before use. Be sure to check at park or forest headquarters on the condition of water sources before depending on them. Droughts, livestock and wildlife use, and other factors can change their status.

Permits

Permits are not usually required to hike in Texas parks and forests, although most have a small park entry fee. Several of the National Park Service areas and state parks allow only day use on certain trails. Generally all National Park Service areas and state parks require you to obtain a permit for overnight trips.

Finding the trailhead

This section provides detailed directions to the trailheads. With a basic current state highway map, you can easily locate the starting point from the directions. In general, the nearest significant town is used as the starting point. Texas has two levels of state highways. The busier, more important roads are designated as Texas highways and use the abbreviation TX in this guide. The smaller, less busy tier of paved state highways is designated as the Farm-to-Market and Ranch-to-Market road system. In this guide I use the common abbreviations FM and RM for these roads.

Distances were measured using a car odometer. Realize that different cars will vary slightly in their measurements. Even the same car will read slightly differently driving uphill on a dirt road versus downhill on a dirt road. Be sure to keep an eye open for the specific signs, junctions, and landmarks mentioned in the directions, not just the mileages. Most of this guide's hikes were selected to have trailheads that could be reached by a sedan. A few, as noted, require high clearance and, except in wet or snowy weather, none usually require a four-wheel drive. Rains or snows can temporarily make some roads impassable. Before venturing onto unimproved dirt roads, you should check with park or forest headquarters. On less-travelled back roads, particularly at Big Bend, you should carry basic emergency equipment, such as a shovel, chains, water, a spare tire, a jack, blankets, and some extra food and clothing. Make sure that your vehicle is in good operating condition with a full tank of gas. Theft and vandalism occasionally occur at trailheads. The local park rangers or sheriff can tell you of any recent problems. Try not to leave valuables in the car at all; if you must, lock them out of sight in the trunk. If I have enough room in the trunk, I usually put everything in to give the car an overall empty appearance. In my many years of parking and hiking at remote trailheads, I have never had my vehicle disturbed.

The hike

All of the hikes selected for this guide can be easily done by people in good physical condition. A little scrambling may be necessary in a few, but none require any rock climbing skills. A few of the hikes, as noted in their descriptions, travel across country or on very faint trails. You should have an experienced hiker, along with a compass and USGS quad, with your group before doing those hikes. The trails are often marked with rock cairns or blazes. Most of the time, the trails are very obvious and easy to follow, but the marks help when the trails are little-used and faint. Cairns are piles of rock built along the route. Tree blazes are i-shaped carvings on trees, usually at shoulder or head height. Be sure not to add your own blazes or cairns; it can confuse the route. Leave such markings to the official trail workers. Possible backcountry campsites are often suggested in the descriptions. Many others are usually available. In the national forests, few restrictions usually exist in selecting a campsite, provided that it is well away from the trail or any water source. Most of the state and national parks require that certain back country campsites be used. The state parks charge a small fee; the national parks do not. After reading the descriptions, pick the hike that appeals most. Go only as far as ability and desire allow. There's no obligation to complete any hike. Remember, you are out hiking to enjoy yourself, not to prove anything.

WILDERNESS ETHICS

A few simple rules and courtesies will help in both preserving the natural environment and allowing others to enjoy their outdoor experience. Every hiker has at least a slight impact on the land and other visitors. Your goal should be to minimize that impact. Some of the rules and suggestions may seen overly restrictive and confining, but with increasing use of shrinking wild areas, such rules have become more necessary. All can be followed with little inconvenience and will contribute to a better outdoor experience for you and others.

Camping

Camp at least 100 yards away from water sources. The vegetation at creeks, lakes, and springs is often the most fragile. Camping well away prevents trampling and destruction of the plant life. Such destruction usually leads to erosion and muddying of water sources. Additionally, camping 100 yards away

The rushing waters of Barton Creek sculpt a limestone ledge.

limits runoff of wash water, food scraps, and human waste. An advantage to dry camps is they are usually warmer and have less insects. Additionally, in desert areas a spring may be the only water source for miles. If you camp too close, you may keep wildlife from reaching water.

Pick a level site that won't require modification to be usable. Don't destroy vegetation in setting up camp. The ideal camp is probably on a bare forest floor carpeted with leaves or pine needles. Don't trench around the tent site. Choose a site with good natural drainage. If possible pick a site that has already been used so that you won't trample another. If you remove rocks, sticks, or other debris, replace them when you depart. You want to leave no trace of your visit when you leave.

Don't pitch your tent right next to someone else's camp. Remember, they are probably out in the woods to get away from people, too. Likewise, set up camp out of sight of trails and avoid creating excessive noise.

If backcountry toilets are available, use them. Many of the state parks have composting or chemical toilets at backcountry campsites. Otherwise, dig a six- to eight-inch-deep hole as far away from water, campsites, and trails as possible and bury human wastes. At that depth, it will quickly decompose. If weather and forest conditions allow, carefully burn toilet paper; otherwise carry it out with you. Fish entrails should be burned or buried. Don't dispose of them in the water.

Carry out all of your trash that hasn't been burned. Remember that those foil freeze-dried food packages won't burn completely. Animals will dig up any garbage that you bury. Food containers are much lighter once the contents have been consumed and are easy to carry. Improve the area for future visitors and take out trash that others have left behind.

Campfires leave permanent scars. If you must build one, do it on bare soil without a fire ring. Use only dead and fallen wood. Put it out thoroughly with water and never leave it unattended. Buried fires can sometimes escape from under the soil. Don't start a fire on dry or windy days. The national forests often limit the use of fires during dry periods. Be sure to honor the restrictions.

Likewise, don't use fires in areas, such the desert, where wood is obviously scarce. For cooking purposes, backpacking stoves are much easier, quicker, and more efficient.

Carry an extra empty gallon jug or wash basin to use for washing yourself or kitchen utensils. Use the jug to carry water and wash well away from the water source to keep soap and other pollutants from flowing into the water.

The trail

Don't shortcut switchbacks on the trail. Switchbacks were built to ease the grade on climbs and to limit erosion. Shortcutting, although it may be shorter, usually takes more effort and unquestionably causes erosion.

Always give horses and other pack animals the right of way. Stand well away from the trail and make no sudden movements or noises that could spook the animals.

If you smoke, stop in a safe spot and make sure that cigarettes and matches are dead out before proceeding. Be sure to take your butts with you. Don't

Hikers need to be sensitive to the fragile nature of the backcountry environment when choosing campsites. Lost Maples State Natural Area.

smoke in windy and dry conditions.

Motorized and mechanized vehicles, including mountain bikes, are prohibited from all wilderness and most national park trails. Other areas may also have restrictions. Some of the state parks have multiple-use trails with hikers, mountain bikers, and horses. Common sense and courtesy will prevent any conflicts.

Don't do anything to disturb the natural environment. Don't cut live trees or plants. Resist the temptation to pick wildflowers. Don't blaze trees, carve initials on rocks, build bridges, or add improvements to campsites. Don't remove any Indian relics or other historic items. All such artifacts are protected by law on government lands.

If you take your dog, please be courteous. Dogs will often annoy other hikers seeking a wilderness experience. Leash him if other hikers are around. Keep him away from water sources to avoid possible pollution. Prevent your dog from disturbing wildlife. Keep him quiet, especially at night. In general, it's probably best to leave your pet at home.

National Parks

Rules in National Park Service areas are generally more restrictive than in other federal lands. Some park areas do not permit backcountry camping. Others require campsites to be located in specific areas. All require that free overnight permits be obtained. Dogs are not allowed on trails, nor may any plants, rocks, or other items be removed. Use of campfires is usually more restricted. Because of perenially dry conditions and lack of wood, Big Bend and Guadalupe Mountains National Parks prohibit the use of campfires altogether. Hunting is prohibited in parks, but fishing is usually permitted with appropriate state licenses.

Other restrictions may apply at certain areas. The local park headquarters and signs at trailheads can inform you of any requirements.

SAFETY

With common sense and good judgment, few mishaps should occur on your hikes. Don't push yourself or companions beyond physical ability. Be aware of changing weather. Know basic first aid techniques.

The following section elaborates on some of the potential hazards that you may encounter on your hikes. Don't let the list scare you. I've been hiking for

All Texas state parks require that permits be obtained for overnight camping.
Colorado Bend State Park.

over twenty years without any serious mishap. The few incidents that have occurred usually were due to carelessness on my part: carrying inadequate water, not using sunscreen, pushing beyond my limits.

Weather

More problems and emergencies in the outdoors are probably related to weather than any other other factor. Even in the hot desert areas, sudden thunderstorms in late summer can drench you, and at the least, make you uncomfortably cool. In the West Texas mountains, temperatures can plummet in storms. When combined with wet clothes or lack of shelter, a life threatening situation can develop.

It's easy to prepare for most weather problems. Always take extra warm clothes, especially on extended hikes. Wool and some synthetics still retain some insulating capability when wet; cotton is worthless. Rain gear is essential, especially on hikes in the mountains in late summer and Central and East Texas in the spring. Carry a reliable tent on the longer hikes. Hole up and wait for the bad weather to pass, rather than attempting a long hike out. Most storms in West Texas, especially in summer, are of short duration. The farther east that you move in the state, the more likely that storms will be longer and wetter.

Hypothermia develops when the body's temperature falls. Texas is generally a warm state, but sudden weather changes, especially in winter and in the mountains, can make hypothermia a risk. If conditions turn wet and cold and a member of your party begins to slur speech, shiver constantly, or becomes clumsy, sleepy, or unreasonable, immediately get the hiker into shelter and out of wet clothes. Give the victim warm liquids to drink and get him into a sleeping bag with one or more people. Skin-to-skin contact conducts body heat to the victim most effectively. This isn't a time for modesty; you may save the victim's life.

At the other extreme, heat can cause problems, particularly in summer in most of the state. On hot weather hikes, carry and drink adequate water. For long hikes in hot weather, plan to carry at least a gallon of water per person per day. Even hikes in the Chisos or Guadalupe Mountains will usually be quite hot in May and June before the summer rains begin. If you do summer hikes, especially in unshaded desert trails in West Texas, try to get an early start to avoid the worst of the heat. Don't push as hard; take frequent breaks; carry lots of water.

With heat exhaustion, the skin is still moist and sweaty, but the victim may feel weak, dizzy, nauseated, or have muscle cramps. Find a cool shady place to rest and feed him plenty of liquids and a few crackers or other source of salt. After the victim feels better, keep him drinking plenty of liquids and limit physical activity. Hike out during a cooler time of day. The condition usually isn't serious, but take the hiker to a doctor as soon as possible.

Heatstroke is less common, but can develop with prolonged exposure to very hot conditions. The body's temperature regulation system stops functioning, resulting in a rapid rise in body temperature. The skin is hot, flushed, and bone-dry.

Confusion and unconsciousness can quickly follow. The situation is life-threatening. Immediately get the victim into the coolest available place.

Remove excess clothes and dampen skin and remaining clothes with water. Fan the victim for additional cooling. If a cool stream or pond is nearby, consider immersing the victim. You must get the body temperature down quickly. Seek medical help immediately.

Lightning poses another threat. When thunderstorms develop, seek lower ground. Stay off hilltops and away from lone trees, lakes, and open areas. Lightning makes exposed mountain peaks and ridges especially hazardous. The most common thunderstorms in the West Texas mountains develop in the afternoons of late summer. Plan to start your hikes early to reach high peaks and ridges by lunch time and head down promptly. The most severe storms usually strike Central and East Texas in the spring. If you get caught in a lightning storm, seek shelter in a low-lying grove of small equal-sized trees if possible. Put down your metal-framed packs, tripods, and metal tent poles and move well away.

Heavy rains can also cause flooding. Stay out of narrow canyons boxed in by cliffs during heavy rains. Even though you may be in sunshine, watch the weather upstream from you. Camp well above and away from streams and rivers. Never camp in that tempting sandy site in the bottom of a dry desert wash. Storms upstream from you can send water sweeping down desert washes with unbelievable fury. In East Texas, broad low-lying floodplains flood regularly. Many of the Big Thicket trails are flooded at least once every spring.

Condition

Good physical condition will not only make your trip safer, but much more pleasant. Don't push yourself too hard, especially at high altitudes. If you have been sedentary for a long time, consider getting a physical exam before starting hiking. Ease into hiking; start with the easy hikes and graduate to more difficult ones. Don't push your party any harder or faster than the weakest member can handle comfortably. Know your limits. When you get tired, rest or turn back. Remember, you are out here to have fun.

Be mentally prepared. Read this guidebook and the specific hike description. Study maps and other books on the area. Every effort has been made to create a guidebook that is as accurate and current as possible, but a few errors may still creep in. Additionally, roads and trails change. Signs can disappear, springs can dry up, roads can wash out, and trails can be rerouted. Talk to park rangers about current road and trail conditions and water sources. Check the weather forecast. Find out the abilities and desires of your hiking companions before hitting the trail.

Altitude

Only a few mountain ranges in West Texas attain very high elevations. Since the highest peak reaches only 8749 feet, most people will have few breathing problems on any of the hikes in Texas. At most, people coming from low elevations may have a little trouble in the higher reaches of the West Texas mountains. Until you acclimatize, you may suffer from a little shortness of breath and tire more easily. A very few hikers may develop headaches, nausea, fatigue, or other mild symptoms such as swelling of the face, hands, ankles, or other body areas at the highest altitudes. Mild symptoms shouldn't change your plans. Rest for a day or two to acclimate. Retreating a thousand feet or so will often clear up any symptoms. Spending several days at moderate altitude before climbing high will often prevent any problems.

Texas's mountains are not high enough to cause the serious symptoms of altitude sickness, such as pulmonary edema (fluid collecting in the lungs) or cerebral edema (fluid accumulating in the brain), except in very rare cases. Should these symptoms develop, immediately get the victim to lower elevations and medical attention.

Companions

Pick your companions wisely. Consider their experience and physical and mental fitness. Try to form groups of relatively similar physical ability. Pick a leader, especially on long trips or with large groups. Ideally, have at least one experienced hiker with the group.

Too large a group is unwieldy and diminishes the wilderness experience for yourself and others. An ideal size is probably four. In case of injury, one can stay with the victim, while the other two can hike out for help. No one is left alone. Leave your travel plans with friends so that they can send help if you do not appear. Allow plenty of time before help is sent; trips often run later than expected.

Never hike alone, especially cross-country or on little-traveled routes. That said, I must confess that I did most of the hikes in this guide alone. However, I religiously informed family or friends of my travel plans on a daily basis and did not deviate from them. Upon returning from a hike I immediately called to let them know that I was back. Never forget to check in at the end of your hike. Nothing will aggravate rescuers more than to find that you were at the local watering hole relaxing with a beer while they were stumbling around in the rain and dark looking for you.

The only time that I did not worry about informing friends of my travel plans was when I did popular hikes on summer weekends. Plenty of other people were on the trail if a mishap had occurred.

Water

Unfortunately, with the heavy use that many back country areas are receiving, all water sources may be contaminated and should be purified before use. Most hikers will not get sick if the water is obtained directly from springs or from streams near their source in little-used areas. However, it is best to play it safe and always treat your water. Boiling vigorously for ten minutes is a reliable method, but slow and consuming of fuel.

Mechanical filtration units are available at most outdoors shops. Filters with a very small pore size strain out bacteria, viruses, cysts, and other microorganisms. Their ability to filter out the smallest organisms, such as viruses, varies from model to model. For very contaminated water, filtration should probably be used in conjunction with chemical treatment.

Chemical treatment is probably the easiest method. Chlorination is the method used by most municipal water systems, but the use of hyperiodide tablets is probably more controllable and reliable for backpackers. They can be purchased at any outdoors store. Follow the directions carefully. Cold or cloudy water requires more chemical use or longer treatment times.

14

The Rio Grande flows out of 1,500-foot deep Santa Elena Canyon in Big Bend National Park.

The cleaner that your water is from the start, the better. Get your water from springs or upstream from trails and camps if possible. For day hikes, it is usually easiest just to carry sufficient water for the day.

Stream crossings

Crossing all but the smallest of streams poses several hazards. Except in flood stage, few of the streams along the trails in this guide are big enough to present much risk of being swept away. However, do not underestimate the power of large bodies of moving water such as the Rio Grande, Pedernales River, Village Creek, or smaller streams in flood. Avoid crossing high volume waterways when possible. If you must cross them, try to find rocks or logs to use, although they may be slippery. Or try to find a broad, slow moving shallow stretch for your ford. Undo the waist strap on your backpack for quick removal if necessary. Use a stout walking stick for stability. Even use a rope if possible.

Since the vast majority of the streams in this guide are too small to sweep you away, the biggest risk probably lies in jumping from rock to rock or crossing on logs to avoid wet feet. Often the rocks or logs are unstable or slippery, making falls very possible. A heavy pack makes such crossings even more tricky. While such a fall might not be life threatening, a twisted ankle or broken leg would present serious problems. Use extra care and assist each other across streams.

Insects

Insects can make or break your trip in some areas at certain times of year. Late spring and summer is the most likely time for problems. Moquitoes will hatch after heavy rains, even in desert regions. In general, mosquitoes and other insects become more of a problem the farther east that you move across the state. A repellant containing DEET in high percentages will discourage mosquitoes and gnats from bothering you. Camp well away from streams, marshes, and other wet areas. Good mosquito netting on your tent will allow a pleasant night's sleep. I have camped many a time in West Texas in dry areas without a tent or netting with no problems at all. However, plan to use tents or netting almost all year on the coastal islands and southeast Texas.

Ticks are common in Central and especially East Texas. They can carry serious diseases, such as Rocky Mountain spotted fever and Lyme disease, so be aware of them. Use insect repellant, wear clothing that fits snugly around the waist, ankles, and wrists, and check yourself and pets every night. If a tick attaches, remove it promptly. Use tweezers and avoid squeezing the tick as you pull it out. Do not leave the head embedded and do not handle the tick. Apply antiseptic to the bite and wash thoroughly. Ticks are probably most common in livestock areas. If you develop any sickness within two or three weeks of the bite, see a doctor.

Fire ants plague most of Central and East Texas year round. Be sure to avoid their small, innocent-seeming mounds or you'll discover the origin of their name.

One of the pleasures of hiking in West Texas is its paucity of nuisance insects.

Bears

Grizzlies have not roamed Texas for decades, so bear attacks are extremely unlikely. Except for a few lone black bears in the Guadalupe Mountains, bears have been virtually extinct in Texas since the 1930s. In the last few years, however, a small number of black bears have begun to re-colonize the Chisos Mountains at Big Bend. The bears have been migrating north from the Sierra del Carmen in Mexico, possibly because of a recent drought in that area. The bears are very scarce, so you are very unlikely to encounter them. If you do, consider yourself lucky. Very few Texans have ever seen a bear in the wild. Give any that you see a wide berth, especially those with cubs.

A few precautions will prevent any problems. Put food and other smelly items, such as soap, toothpaste, and garbage, into a stuffsack and hang it from a tree well away from your tent. Hang it at least ten feet above the ground and out from the trunk. Let it dangle a few feet below the limb to prevent access from above. Hanging your food up will also discourage rodents and raccoons. Leave your packs unzipped to prevent damage to them by a nosy animal. Never cook in your tent or keep food in your tent or sleeping bag. If a bear does take your food, don't even think about trying to get it back.

The mountain lions in the Chisos Mountains have lost some of their fear of humans after years of no hunting. On rare occasions, hikers have encountered them on the trail. If you do see a lion, you are very fortunate. If they don't immediately run away, stand your ground or retreat slowly. Don't act like prey by running away or screaming. Check with park rangers for more advice on handling such an encounter.

Snakes

The vast majority of snakes that you will encounter (usually you will see none) are nonpoisonous. On rare occasions you may encounter a rattlesnake.

Most are not aggressive and will not strike unless stepped on or otherwise provoked. In daytime or cold weather they are usually holed up under rocks and in cracks. The most likely time to see them is in summer evenings in Central and West Texas. If you watch your step, don't hike at night, and don't put your hands or feet under rocks, ledges, and other places that you can't see, you should never have any problem. Don't hurt or kill any that you find. Remember, they are important predators.

Texas also has water moccasins, copperheads, and coral snakes, particularly the farther east that you move across the state. All will be seen only on rare occasions. They will not usually be aggressive and will seek to avoid conflicts, similar to the rattlesnakes.

If bitten, get medical help as soon as possible. Treatment methods are very controversial and beyond the scope of this book. Fortunately, the majority of bites do not inject a significant amount of venom. For basic treatment, tie a shoelace or other cord around the affected extremity between the bite and the rest of the body. Tie it only tight enough to dent the skin; don't cut off blood circulation. Apply ice if available. Get to a doctor. Do not use a snakebite kit unless you are very far from medical help.

Equipment

The most important outdoor equipment is probably your footwear. Hiking boots should be sturdy and comfortable. The lightweight boots are probably adequate for all but rugged trails and routes and for carrying heavy packs. Proper clothing, plenty of food and water, and a pack are other necessities. Other vital items for every trip include waterproof matches, raingear or some sort of emergency shelter, a pocketknife, a signal mirror and whistle, a first-aid kit, a detailed map, and a compass.

In general, all of your outdoor equipment should be as light and small as possible. Many excellent books and outdoor shops will help you select the proper boots, tents, sleeping bags, cooking utensils, and other equipment necessary for your hikes.

Getting lost

Careful use of the maps and hike descriptions should prevent you from ever getting lost. However, if you should become lost or disoriented, immediately stop. Charging around blindly will only worsen the problem. Careful study of the map, compass, and surrounding landmarks will often reorient you. If you can retrace your route, follow it until you are oriented again. Don't proceed unless you are sure of your location. If you left travel plans with friends or family, rescuers should find you soon. In an emergency, follow a drainage downstream. In most areas, it will eventually lead you to a trail, road, or town. Remember, however, that it will probably take you farther away from rescuers. In a few of the largest wild areas, in particular the Guadalupe Mountains and Big Bend, it may take you deeper into the backcountry before finally leading out.

Because of good trails and open country, people are unlikely to get lost on most of the hikes in this guide. Be careful, however, if you leave the trail in the dense woods and flat terrain of East Texas. It's very easy to become disoriented. However, the wild areas of East Texas are generally quite small. Following a drainage will usually bring you to a road, residence, or town fairly quickly.

Use of signals may help rescuers find you. A series of three flashes or noises is the universal distress signal. Use the whistle or signal mirror. Provided that it can be done safely, a small smoky fire may help rescuers find you.

Hunting

The national forests generally allow hunting during the various seasons set up by state agencies. Fall in particular can bring out large numbers of deer hunters. The seasons vary from year to year and in different parts of the state. Check with local ranger stations before your hike to determine what if any seasons might be in effect. If you hike during a hunting season, inquire locally to find areas that are less popular with hunters and wear bright colored clothing. Most of the state parks and National Park Service areas do not allow hunting.

HIKING WITH CHILDREN

Don't be afraid to take your children with you the next time that you take a hiking trip. Kids of almost any age will enjoy hiking if they aren't pushed beyond their ability. Babies and small toddlers can be carried in specially designed backpacks. As children get older and too large to carry, plan easy hikes that fit within their physical limits. If children are pushed too hard, not only will they (and you) be miserable, they may develop a long term aversion to hiking and the outdoors.

Be sure to bring plenty of snacks for your children and take lots of rest breaks. Carry adequate clothing for any possible weather extreme. Children are much smaller than adults and will get chilled and possibly hypothermic much more quickly than adults if the weather suddenly turns wet or cold. Don't forget to carry insect repellent, especially on hikes in the central and eastern parts of the state. You may be tough enough to handle a few mosquitoes, but they will quickly make your kids miserable.

Most children are curious and will get excited when taken to a new place. However, in their excitement, they may run off in all directions. To avoid getting separated, be sure to watch them at all times. Young children, in particular, do not appreciate the dangers posed by cliffs, fast-flowing rivers, poison ivy, and other hazards.

Teach your children ahead of time what to do in case they do get separated from you. Have them stay in one place until they are found. If they always carry a whistle with them, they may be able to lead you right to them. Show them how to avoid snakes and identify poison ivy.

Plan shorter hikes than you would normally take without children. Pick hikes that have extras that will interest them. Many of the hikes in this guide follow permanent streams. Water always seems to attract children; before you know it your kids will be wading, skipping rocks, or building dams. Sand dunes and caves will also appeal. Be sure to supervise them closely.

The following hikes should entice children. A few may be difficult if hiked in their entirety, but most are easy and all are interesting even if only hiked a short distance.

You can't lose taking children of any age to Monahans Sandhills (Hike #29). Of course you may spend the next two days getting the sand out of everything.

The rocks and boulders at Hueco Tanks (Hike #24) will entertain children for hours. Likewise, the granite domes of Enchanted Rock (Hike #30) will have great appeal. Watch carefully, though. There are very high cliffs at both parks and the many boulders and crevices make it easy for kids to slip out of sight.

Both the short, easy Sundew Trail (Hike #73) and the longer Kirby Trail (Hike #74) in the Big Thicket are nature trails that will teach your children about the natural environment.

Some good hikes along streams include the Sawmill Trail in East Texas (Hike #66), Lost Maples in the Hill Country (Hike #35), and the Window (Hike #3) at Big Bend National Park. Remember, on the Window hike the trail is uphill all the way back to the trailhead. Make sure that your kids are strong enough to hike back without becoming exhausted.

Smith Spring (Hike #20) is an easy hike to a shady oasis in the Guadalupe Mountains. The spring is very delicate, though, so you will need to keep your children out of the water on this hike. Palmetto (Hike #43) is a very easy hike in central Texas.

Hamilton Pool (Hike #50) is a sure winner. The high point of this easy Hill Country hike is the large, natural swimming hole partially roofed by a cave. Pedernales Falls (Hike #33) has a good wading and swimming area only a short distance into the hike. The beaches of Padre Island (Hike #46) and Matagorda Island (Hike #44) will be popular. Watch you children closely when they are in or near the water. Don't let them dive in these natural swimming areas of uncertain depth.

THE HIKES

Backpackers look far into Mexico from the South Rim of the Chisos Mountains.

HIKE 1: *SOUTH RIM*

General description: A strenuous overnight trip to the South Rim of the Chisos Mountains

General location: Big Bend National Park

Length: About 14.5 miles round trip

Elevation: 5,400 to 7,460 feet

Maps: Big Bend National Park topo map, Big Bend National Park "Trails Illustrated" topo map, The Basin and Emory Peak 7.5-minute USGS quads

Best season: All year

Water availability: Seasonal at Boot Spring, trailhead

Special attractions: Views, rare birds and plants

Permit: Required for camping

Finding the trailhead: From park headquarters at Panther Junction in Big Bend National Park, drive west on the road toward the Basin and Santa Elena Canyon. Turn left (south) at about three miles onto the Basin road. Stop at the large parking area at the lodge at the end of the road after almost seven additional miles.

The hike: The South Rim is probably the classic hike of Texas. Although the trip is fairly strenuous, almost any Texas hiker worth his salt will someday try to hike to the South Rim. Few other hikes in Texas can surpass the quality and sheer quantity of views along the trail. On clear days, the views cover most of the Texas Big Bend country and far into Mexico.

To fully enjoy the trip try to allow two or three days. For people in good shape, however, the hike can be done in one day. It can be shortened by about 2.3 miles by skipping the East Rim. Not surprisingly, the hike is popular. Although there are many designated primitive campsites, it may be difficult to reserve one during Thanksgiving or college spring break.

The described route is a loop. It is less steep to do the loop in reverse from what I describe; however, for backpackers planning to get water at Boot Spring, I recommend that you do the loop as described. Be sure to check on the spring's status before you start—it does dry up sometimes. If it is flowing, it will save carrying part of your water up the bulk of the climb.

The trail starts from the bottom of the parking lot and immediately hits a three-way junction. As with all the trail junctions in the Chisos Mountains, this one is well-marked. Go left, towards the Pinnacles Trail and the South Rim. The trail forks again in a short distance; go left toward Emory Peak on the Pinnacles Trail. You'll pass several lodge cabins and a water tank. Ignore the Chisos Basin Loop trail forking right after about .5 mile.

The trail levels out for breathers at Juniper Flat and Boulder Meadow, but generally keeps climbing at a moderate, but unrelenting grade. After switchbacking steeply up the rocky wall of the Basin, the trail tops out with great views back down the way you came. If you're lucky, you may see some beautiful fall maples in October along the trail a little below the top.

After reaching the top, the trail starts down a tributary of Boot Canyon, passing the Emory Peak Trail on the right (See Hike #4). After about a mile, the Colima Trail forks to the right. Stay left toward the South Rim. The trail passes the corral and Park Service cabin. To find the spring, go down the slope behind the cabin a short distance on an unmarked trail. Use as little water as possible; wildlife depends on it, too. Be sure to purify the water.

Boot Canyon is home to the Colima warbler, a Mexican bird that only lives in the U.S. in the Chisos Mountains. Similarly, the wilted-looking tree, the Mexican drooping juniper, that grows in the canyon occurs only in the Chisos Mountains. The canyon is one of the lushest areas of the park, with Arizona cypress, bigtooth maple, and even a few ponderosa pines and Douglas firs.

Ignore the Juniper Canyon trail that forks off to the left a little past the spring. After another .5 mile, the trail forks again. Turn left and follow the trail to the East Rim. If you are tired or short on time, go right, straight to the South Rim. By going right, you will cut off over two miles, but will miss one of the most scenic parts of the hike. At certain times of the year, you will have to go right. If peregrine falcons are roosting at the East Rim, the Park Service closes it from about February to July.

The trail to the East Rim makes a spectacular loop out along the edge of the East and South rims before rejoining the shorter right fork on the rim. Continue along the rim past the junction. The trail eventually turns back north away from the rim. After 1.5 miles or so, the trail passes the Colima Trail on the right and then, a short distance later, the Blue Creek Trail on the left.

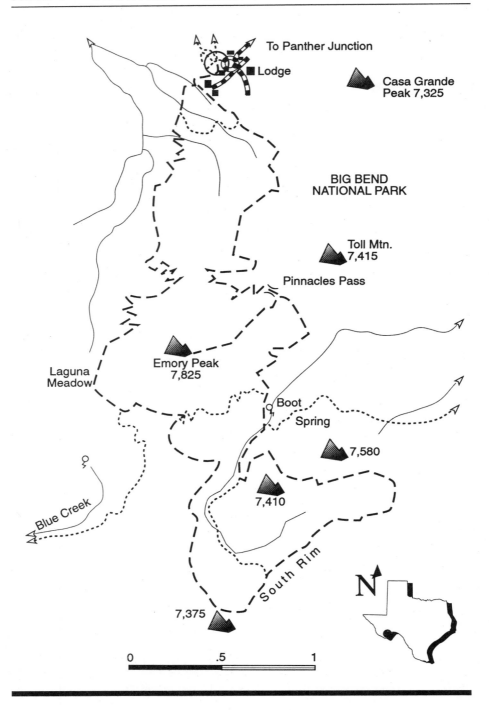

To Panther Junction

Lodge

Casa Grande
Peak 7,325

BIG BEND
NATIONAL PARK

Toll Mtn.
7,415

Pinnacles Pass

Emory Peak
7,825

Laguna
Meadow

Boot
Spring

7,580

7,410

Blue Creek

South Rim

7,375

N

0   .5   1

After the Blue Creek junction, the trail passes through Laguna Meadow, a lush grassy valley with scattered pines and junipers. After the meadow, the trail begins the long descent back into the Basin and back to your car.

The hike will be hot in summer, but is high and wooded enough to be enjoyable. Get an early start for the climb out of the Basin. The trail is also good in winter, but be prepared for the occasional winter storm. The mountains will usually get a few snows, but they are usually light and short-lived.

HIKE 2: *LOST MINE TRAIL*

General description: A moderate day hike to one of the most spectacular views in Texas
General location: Big Bend National Park
Length: About five miles round trip
Elevation: 5,760-6,850 feet
Maps: Big Bend National Park topo map, Big Bend National Park "Trails Illustrated" topo map, The Basin 7.5-minute USGS quad
Best season: All year
Water availability: None
Special attractions: Views
Finding the trailhead: From Big Bend National Park headquarters at Panther Junction, drive west toward Alpine and the Basin. At about three miles, turn left, south, onto the marked paved road to the Basin. After about 5.4 miles, the road

Casa Grande Peak is one of the most distinctive peaks in the Chisos Mountains.

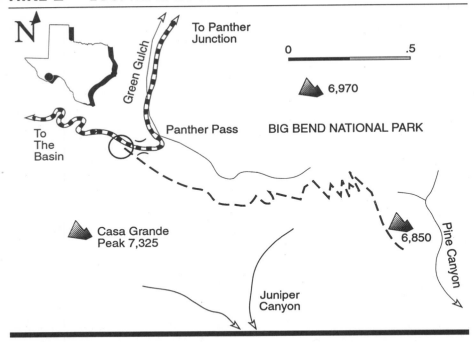

reaches a pass before dropping down into the Basin. Park in the large parking lot at the top of the pass.

The hike: The Lost Mine Trail is one of the most popular hikes at Big Bend for good reason. The trail requires less climbing and is considerably shorter than the South Rim Trail but provides views that are almost as spectacular. Lost Mine Peak, rising above the promontory at the end of the trail, was named for an old Spanish legend. Supposedly, at certain times of the year, the rising sun shines on the entrance of a rich mine developed by the old Spaniards. Unfortunately, the Chisos Mountains are not geologically predisposed to mineralization, making the legend probably only a fanciful story.

The trail climbs steeply southeast from the parking lot on a paved surface. Within 100 feet or so, the pavement ends and the grade moderates. An interesting self-guiding booklet is available at the trailhead.

The first mile of the hike climbs gradually up to a saddle between Juniper Canyon and Green Gulch. The trail passes through pinyon-juniper-oak forest, with the beautiful red-barked Texas madrone mixed in. The drooping juniper appears permanently wilted and occurs in the United States only in the Chisos Mountains.

The view from the saddle is spectacular and worthy of a trip in itself. However, it is only a warm-up for the view from the top. A primitive route climbs from the saddle to the southwest to the summit of Casa Grande Peak. The route is difficult and should only be attempted by expert hikers. Casa Grande Peak is usually closed from February to July to avoid disturbing nesting peregrine falcons.

After the saddle, the trail begins to climb at a steeper grade, with numerous switchbacks up a less-wooded southwest-facing slope. At roughly two miles, the trail tops out on a ridge and follows it, ending on a spectacular rocky promontory at about 2.4 miles. Views stretch in all directions, from the surrounding peaks of the Chisos Mountains to the high peaks of the Sierra del Carmen far to the southeast in Mexico. In the canyon below the ridge, a few ponderosa pines manage to survive in the dry mountains. Since the Park Service doesn't allow camping on the Lost Mine Trail, consider carrying a good flashlight so that you can watch the sunset over the mountains before descending.

The hike can be hot, but not unbearable, in summer. Rare snows will hit in winter, but overall the trail is good year round. Be aware of lightning, especially during the afternoon thunderstorms of late summer. The hike is one of my favorites in Texas.

Sotol plants dot Green Gulch in the Chisos Mountains at Big Bend National Park.

HIKE 3: *THE WINDOW*

General description: A moderate day hike to a narrow rock gorge and seasonal 200-foot waterfall
General location: Big Bend National Park
Length: About 5.2 miles round trip
Elevation: 5,400-4,400 feet
Maps: Big Bend National Park topo map, Big Bend National Park "Trails Illustrated" topo map, The Basin 7.5-minute USGS quad
Best season: All year
Water availability: Trailhead, seasonal at Window
Special attractions: Narrow rocky gorge, waterfall
Finding the trailhead: See Hike #1, the South Rim

The hike: The Basin is a large, partially wooded valley in the heart of the Chisos Mountains. Few people who see the sheer ramparts of the mountains from below suspect the presence of such a valley. Much of the Basin is ringed by cliffs and high peaks. Wildlife favors the valley because the extra rain fosters more lush vegetation than grows in the desert below.

The Window is the prominent gap in the encircling cliffs of the basin. All creeks and washes in the valley funnel through the narrow cut at the Window.

HIKE 3 *THE WINDOW*

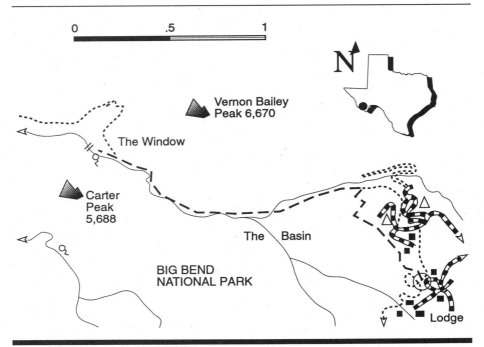

This trail starts at the lodge area at the upper end of the Basin and goes west, downhill across the Basin floor to the Window.

From the large main parking area at the lodge and store, go to the main trailhead at the west side of the lot. The trail starts as a concrete sidewalk, but several trails split off within a few yards. Go right toward the Window, as marked. The trail immediately splits again; go left toward the Window (not the campground).

The trail descends steadily, passing initially through thick grasses and scattered pinyon pine and juniper. After a short distance, the trail passes the riding stables (the flies will let you know) and the group campground. The terrain becomes drier and continues to descend at a moderate grade. At about .5 mile, a trail forks back right, uphill, to the main campground. Continue downhill to the left. The next mile or so has little shade and is hot in summer, especially on the uphill return trip.

The trees, oaks in particular, become more common when the trail meets the junction of two of the main basin drainages. The valley quickly narrows, forming a sheer-walled canyon of reddish volcanic rock. In wet years, the stream will flow through the entire length of the gorge. In most years, the stream appears only after passing through a particularly narrow twist in the canyon. Shortly before the end, a side trail climbs off to the right that goes around the waterfall and drops down to Oak Spring and the desert below. After reaching the hitching rails for horses, the trail enters a cool, narrow gorge. Steps carved and built in the rock make it possible to continue a short distance further. In wet years or after heavy rains, the crystal-clear water cascades down from pool to pool. Usually a tiny stream flows through the Window, except in the driest years. The gorge ends abruptly at the top of a 200-foot waterfall, one of the highest in Texas. Don't go too close to the lip; the water-polished rock is wet and slippery.

If you use the water, be sure to purify it first. The trail gets heavy use by people and horses. Be wary during stormy weather; heavy rains can send flood waters roaring through the narrow gorge.

HIKE 4: *EMORY PEAK*

General description: A strenuous day hike to the highest peak in the Chisos Mountains
General location: Big Bend National Park
Length: About nine miles round trip
Elevation: 5,400-7,825 feet
Maps: Big Bend National Park topo map, Big Bend National Park "Trails Illustrated" topo map, The Basin and Emory Peak 7.5-minute USGS quads
Best season: All year
Water availability: None
Special attractions: Views, maples
Permit: Required for camping
Finding the trailhead: See Hike #1, the South Rim.

Large century plants, or agaves, grow throughout the Chisos Mountains.

The hike: Emory Peak towers over the south side of the Basin, forming the highest peak in the Chisos Mountains. Much of the mountains are igneous rhyolite, formed from molten rock. The line of peaks from Casa Grande to Emory Peak formed when lava squeezed up out of the earth onto the surface. The flows cooled quickly, forming deep cracks in the rock. As time passed, erosion along these cracks and joints formed sheer walls, buttresses, and pinnacles.

From the parking lot, take the trail marked for Laguna Meadow, the Pinnacles, and the South Rim. The trail goes south, below the motel units. In a few hundred yards, the trail forks below the old stone cabins of the lodge. Go left, uphill, on the Pinnacles Trail toward Emory Peak. The right fork goes to Laguna Meadow. The trail climbs up right past the cabins and onto a steep gravel service road. Follow up the road a short distance, as marked by the signs. The trail quickly branches off to the left and around a water tank, the road's destination.

The route climbs steadily through a dense pinyon-juniper-oak woodland. Along the way the trail passes several small side-trails. These go only a short distance to designated backcountry campsites. Usually they are marked by unobtrusive signs with initials and a number. At a little over .5 mile, the marked Chisos Basin Loop trail forks right. Stay left on the main trail. The flat, grassy meadow of Juniper Flat gives a nice break in the steady climb at about a mile. Boulder Meadow, a nice easy day day hike destination, is passed at about 1.5 miles.

After Boulder Meadow, the trail begins to switchback steeply up the south wall of the basin. Just below the top, the trail passes through a stand of bigtooth maples. The trees turn gold and scarlet in fall, producing some of the best color in Texas in good years.

Finally, after much sweating, you reach the crest at Pinnacles Pass, a bit less than 3.5 miles from the trailhead. The trail drops down over the pass into a branch of Boot Canyon. After only a short distance, the marked trail to Emory Peak forks to the right. The one-mile trail to the peak immediately begins climbing again, passing through a small, recent forest fire along the way. Views become more and more impressive as you progress. The last few feet involve a scramble up a rock wall onto the craggy summit. The Park Service radio transmitters on a secondary summit are obnoxious but necessary. Use care on top. Sheer drops lie on most sides of the peak. On clear days the views are tremendous, from the Davis Mountains near Alpine and Marfa to mountains over one hundred miles away in Mexico. Unfortunately, smog, largely from unrestricted pollution in Mexico, often limits the view.

In late summer, afternoon thunderstorms are common in the Chisos Mountains. The summit and the last mile of trail are very exposed, so plan to get an early start so that you can be coming down by early afternoon. The hike can be fairly hot in summer, but there is plenty of shade. Occasional winter storms drop snow on the Chisos Mountains and temperatures can fall well below freezing, so be prepared.

Ideally, plan to camp at one of the primitive campsites near the peak—be sure to obtain a permit ahead of time—and then watch one of the best sunsets in Texas from the summit.

HIKE 5: *DOG CANYON*

General description: An easy day hike into a deep, sheer-walled canyon
General location: Big Bend National Park
Length: About five miles round trip
Elevation: 2,570-2,520 feet
Maps: Big Bend National Park topo map, Big Bend National Park "Trails Illustrated" topo map, Dagger Flat and Bone Spring 7.5-minute USGS quads
Best season: Fall through spring
Water availability: None
Special attractions: Deep narrow canyon.
Finding the trailhead: From Big Bend National Park headquarters at Panther Junction, drive north on the road to Marathon about twenty-four miles (or south 3.6 miles from the Persimmon Gap visitor center) to the highway pullout with the Dog Canyon interpretive sign. The pullout is about .25 mile north of the bridge over Bone Spring Draw.

The hike: Dog Canyon is the obvious cut in the ridge to the east of the trailhead. Bone Spring and Nine Point Draws drain the large valley on the north side of the park. The draw has carved the canyon through the Dead Horse Mountains over the course of millennia. The Dead Horse Mountains are a rugged desert mountain range that begins north of the park and rises to the south. The mountains are notable for their lack of springs or seeps. Dog Canyon provides

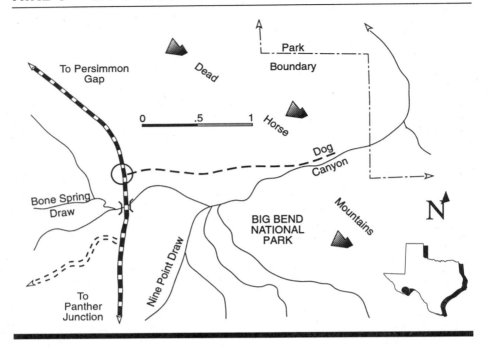

one of the few easy passages through the mountains. The mountains are an extension of the towering Sierra del Carmen of Mexico, separated only by Boquillas Canyon, a deep canyon of the Rio Grande. In Mexico, the mountains reach 9,000 feet and are heavily wooded with pine, fir, and aspen. The Mexican government plans to designate the Sierra del Carmen as a national park, twin to Big Bend.

No formal trail exists, but the route to the canyon is easy. Just walk straight toward the canyon from the parking lot across the creosote flats. Generally only scattered clumps of creosote and few cacti and clumps of grass grow on the flats, making walking easy. Traces of an old road come and go on the route. The flats used to be good grasslands, but overgrazing before creation of the park destroyed the vegetation. Rains washed away the topsoil, leaving little but bare ground and creosote, even after almost fifty years of no grazing.

Shortly before reaching the canyon, drop into the wash and follow it into the canyon. The thick layers of Santa Elena limestone forming the walls are folded and faulted into a large overturned anticline. After a short distance, the canyon opens back up into another large valley. The park boundary lies only 200 yards beyond the canyon.

The hike is very hot in summer, with no shade along the route until you reach the canyon. Be careful if rain is likely. A very large area drains through the narrow slot of Dog Canyon, making it an unhealthy place to be during flash floods.

HIKE 6: *GRAPEVINE HILLS*

General description: An easy day hike to a wonderland of rock formations
General location: Big Bend National Park
Length: About 2.2 miles round trip
Elevation: 3,230-3,480 feet
Maps: Big Bend National Park topo map, Big Bend National Park "Trails Illustrated" topo map, Grapevine Hills 7.5-minute USGS quad
Best season: Fall through spring
Water availability: None
Special attractions: Natural stone arch, granite boulders
Finding the trailhead: From Big Bend National Park headquarters at Panther Junction, drive west about three miles toward Alpine and the Basin. Just past the paved Basin turnoff on the left, turn right, or north, on the gravel Grapevine Hills road. The road has a good gravel surface for the first four or five miles. The last couple of miles are rougher, but with care, usually passable by any vehicle. The parking area is on the right, in a canyon mouth, at about seven miles. A small plaque marks the parking area. If you miss the turnoff, don't worry. The road only goes another mile before ending at Grapevine Spring.

The hike: The Grapevine Hills were formed when molten rock, or magma, pooled and hardened underground in a large lens-shaped body called a

HIKE 6   *GRAPEVINE HILLS*

A stone arch lies at the end of the Grapevine Hills Trail.

laccolith. Erosion exposed the laccolith to the surface. The exposed granite has weathered into a fanciful jumble of boulders and pinnacles.

The trail follows the canyon bottom upstream for almost a mile before a short climb up to a small pass or saddle. Except for the short climb at the end, the trail grade is mild. Walking in the soft sand of the desert wash is the only difficulty. Once you reach the crest of the small pass, follow the trail up the ridge to the right, or west. The trail can be a bit hard to follow through the boulders along the ridge, but metal fence posts and signs help mark the way. In about 100 yards the trail ends at a photogenic arch formed by two pinnacles and a boulder.

Although the trail is short, the rock formations invite additional exploration throughout the hills. The desert hike can be very hot from about April through September. Be sure to go early or late in the day during those months, and carry plenty of water.

HIKE 7: *THE CHIMNEYS*

General description: An easy day hike to a prominent rock landmark
General location: Big Bend National Park
Length: About five miles round trip
Elevation: 3,180-2,800 feet
Maps: Big Bend National Park topo map, Big Bend National Park "Trails Illustrated" topo map, Cerro Castellan 7.5-minute USGS quad

HIKE 7   *THE CHIMNEYS*

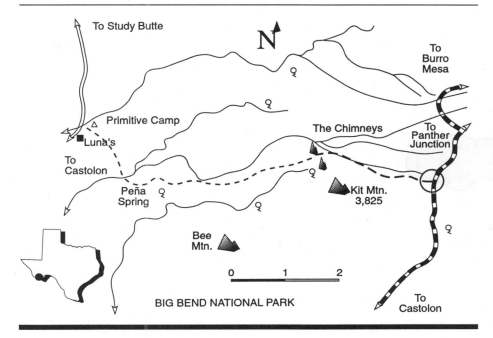

Best season: Fall through spring
Water availability: None
Special attractions: Views, petroglyphs
Finding the trailhead: From Big Bend National Park headquarters at Panther Junction, go about thirteen miles west on the road to Alpine and Study Butte. Turn left on the paved road to Santa Elena Canyon and Castolon. Go about 13.2 miles to the small parking area on the right, or west, side of the road (about 1.2 miles beyond the Burro Mesa Pouroff turnoff). A small sign marks the Chimneys Trail.

The hike: The tall ridge of rock outcrops known as the Chimneys has been a landmark for hundreds of years. Indian petroglyphs decorate one rock wall and the remains of small rock shelters used by herders are tucked against the rocks. The Chimneys are visible from the trailhead as a long rocky ridge down the long slope to the west. They appear closer than the 2.4 miles away that they are. The good trail follows a fairly straight route across the desert flats to the Chimneys. The ridge is in sight for virtually the entire hike. The trail slopes slightly downhill for the whole hike, resulting in a gentle climb on the return trip.

The Chimneys are reached at a little less than 2.5 miles. The petroglyphs are on a wall of the southernmost rock tower. Please don't disturb or deface them. Be sure to scramble up to the top of the rocky ridge for an endless view of desert and distant mountains.

The Chimneys hike is very hot in summer, with little shade along the route. With a car shuttle (or a long round trip hike), the trail can be continued west, past the Chimneys to the Old Maverick Road. The seven-mile one-way hike makes an excellent winter trip. The trail hits Old Maverick Road just north of Luna's Jacal. To extend the hike a shorter distance, walk cross-country about 1.5 miles northwest of the Chimneys to Red Ass Spring, marked by a large cottonwood tree.

HIKE 8: *ERNST TINAJA*

General description: A very easy day hike to a desert waterhole
General location: Big Bend National Park
Length: About one-mile round trip
Elevation: 2190-2310 feet
Maps: Big Bend National Park topo map, Big Bend National Park "Trails Illustrated" topo map, Roys Peak 7.5-minute USGS quad
Best season: Fall through spring
Water availability: See text
Special attractions: Contorted multi-colored rock layers, permanent desert water hole
Finding the trailhead: From Big Bend National Park headquarters, go east on the road to Rio Grande Village about fifteen miles to the marked Old Ore Road turnoff on the left. The Old Ore Road is rough and requires a high clearance vehicle to get to the tinaja trailhead. Follow the ore road north about 4.5 miles to the bottom of a large drainage. Turn right, or east, onto the Ernst Tinaja spur road and go .5 mile to the parking lot at the road's end. Be sure to inquire about the ore road's condition before your trip. The road washes out regularly and is

A sandstone butte lies below the Chisos Mountains of Big Bend National Park.

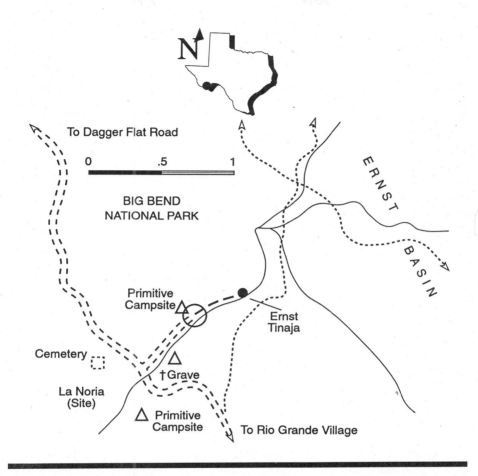

only maintained on occasion. With care, passenger cars can sometimes make the first three miles of the road.

The hike: Ernst Tinaja is one of the few sources of water in the Dead Horse Mountains. Tinaja is the Spanish word used for a natural stone waterhole. Ernst Tinaja lies in a canyon that drains a large basin in the desert mountains. Over the eons, flowing water has carved a deep rock tank in the bottom of the canyon that periodic rains and floods refill. Possibly a small spring adds water to the tinaja, because it never dries up. The tinaja is an important water source for wildlife. When the water level gets low, animals sometimes drown in the tank because they are unable to climb out.

From the parking area, walk up the dry desert canyon bottom about .5 mile to the tinaja. The canyon narrows and the walls rise as you approach the tank. The cliffs at the tank are part of the Ernst Member of the Boquillas Formation.

The thin layers of limestone and shale form a layer about 450 feet thick. The multiple layers, colored yellow, white, dull red, and pale lavender, are twisted and contorted enough to make a taffy maker green with envy.

Be sure to hike up the canyon beyond the tinaja. The canyon continues to narrow and deepen, forming a slot canyon reminiscent of the slick rock country of Utah, lacking only the red coloration. The hike to the tinaja is very short and easy, but one of my favorites at Big Bend. The hike is very hot in summer, but the canyon walls provide quite a bit of shade. Be careful if rain threatens, especially in late summer, because the narrow canyon could be a trap in a flash flood. Plan to carry your own water for this short hike. Water can be obtained from the tinaja, but even with purification, it is of questionable quality.

HIKE 9: SANTA ELENA CANYON

General description: An easy day hike into the mouth of one of the main canyons of the Rio Grande
General location: Big Bend National Park
Length: About 1.7 miles round trip
Elevation: 2,160-2,240 feet
Maps: Big Bend National Park topo map, Big Bend National Park "Trails Illustrated" topo map, Castolon 7.5-minute USGS quad
Best season: Fall through spring
Water availability: None, see text
Special attractions: 1,500-feet deep canyon
Finding the trailhead: From park headquarters at Panther Junction, go west on the Alpine road about thirteen miles to the Castolon and Santa Elena junction. Go left (south) on the Castolon road for about thirty miles to the end of the paved road at the Santa Elena Canyon parking area.

The hike: Santa Elena Canyon is the first of three major canyons cut by the Rio Grande in Big Bend National Park. The narrow seven-mile long canyon slices through the thick limestone layers of the Mesa de Anguila. The canyon walls rise in sheer cliffs as much as 1,500 feet from the river to the rim above. Peregrine falcons nest in impossible aeries high above the muddy Rio Grande. Rafters float Santa Elena Canyon more than any other stretch of the Rio Grande in the park. The canyon ends abruptly at the mouth, across from the parking area.

Follow the popular trail from the parking lot through a dense thicket of cane, mesquite, willow, and tamarisk to the confluence of Terlingua Creek and the Rio Grande. Depending on rainfall and the amount of gravel deposited at the confluence, you may have to wade across Terlingua Creek to continue the hike up into the canyon. If the creek is flowing deep or fast, wait until another day to complete the hike.

Across the creek the trail switchbacks up a rocky bluff into the canyon before slowly descending back to the river bank. The trail winds through house-sized boulders and dense thickets of cane before ending where the river cuts off the river bank at the canyon wall.

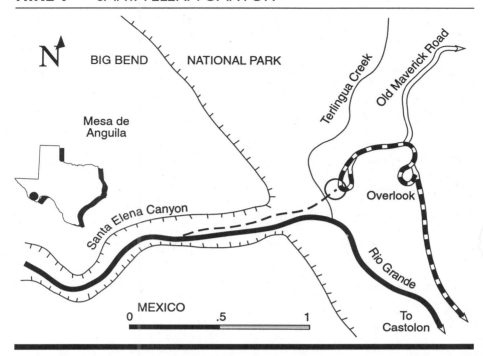

The hike is very hot in summer, but except at mid-day, the canyon walls and cane thickets provide good shade. As tempting as it may look, be wary about swimming in the Rio Grande. As the river hisses by with no rapids, it appears inviting on hot days. However, its placid appearance belies considerable depth and strong currents. Plan to carry water for your hike; river and creek water is marginal even with purification. Keep an eye on the weather, especially in late summer. If Terlingua Creek floods, you will be trapped in the canyon. Be sure to note the 1990 high-water mark way up on the bathroom wall at the parking lot.

HIKE 10: *MARISCAL MOUNTAIN*

General description: A moderately strenuous day hike to the rim of Mariscal Canyon

General location: Big Bend National Park

Length: About 6.6 miles round trip

Elevation: 1980-3260 feet

Maps: Big Bend National Park topo map, Big Bend National Park "Trails Illustrated" topo map, Mariscal Mountain 7.5-minute USGS quad

Best season: Late fall through early spring

Water availability: None

Special attractions: Spectacular views of Mariscal Canyon

Finding the trailhead: From park headquarters at Panther Junction, take the paved road southeast to Rio Grande Village. At about fifteen miles, turn right onto the marked River Road. A high clearance vehicle is usually necessary to traverse the dirt River Road. After heavy rains the road may be impassable or require a four-wheel drive vehicle. Be sure to inquire at headquarters before starting this trip. Follow the River Road for about twenty-three miles to the Talley turnoff on the left. Before reaching the Talley turnoff, you will pass several side roads to old fishing camps and primitive campsites. The Glenn Spring and Black Gap roads forking off to the right make alternate return routes, although the Black Gap road is very rough. Follow the Talley road about six miles to the trailhead. Stop in the parking area up on the bank above the floodplain. Talley can also be reached by following the River Road from the west, but the route is much rougher. Don't leave any valuables (or ideally anything) in your vehicle. Cars are broken into periodically by Mexicans crossing the river.

The hike: The Rio Grande cuts through Mariscal Mountain, forming the narrowest canyon in the park. Its sheer walls tower 1,300 feet above the river. Peregrine falcons drift high above the water, searching for prey. Mercury ore was discovered in 1900 on the north side of Mariscal Mountain, and mines were

HIKE 10 *MARISCAL MOUNTAIN*

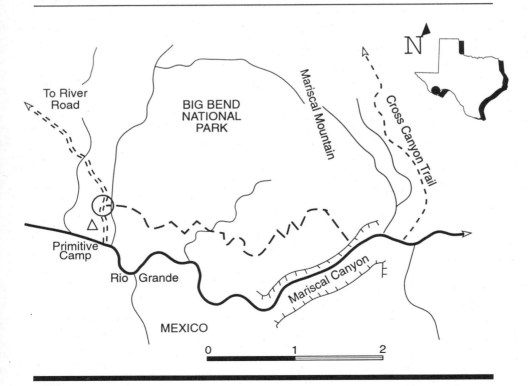

worked sporadically until 1943. The River Road passes the ruins of the mines on the way to Talley.

The trail is little-used, so you are unlikely to see anyone else on your hike. The first two miles of the trail are easy as it crosses the flats and gentle slopes at the base of the mountain. The trail then begins the steep, rocky climb to the top of Mariscal Mountain. The stark, cactus-covered desert slopes climb with little relief until you reach the crest. A short walk southeast across the top brings you, sweating and panting, to the sheer lip of the spectacular canyon. Be careful on the edge; there's nothing between you and the river but air. On occasion, you may see the tiny dot of a raft as it negotiates the Tight Squeeze.

This is not a summer hike. I made the trip in mid-April at high noon and was toasted in 100+ degree temperatures. There is no shade. Three liters of water was not enough to get me through the entire hike in properly hydrated condition. The rugged, isolated trail is best done by experienced hikers. The warnings said, don't miss this spectacular, little-traveled trail. With a topo map, expert hikers can continue cross-country to the Cross Canyon Trail and descend to the river in the heart of the canyon.

HIKE 11: ROSILLOS PEAK

General description: A very strenuous cross-country day hike to the top of the Rosillos Mountains
General location: Big Bend National Park
Length: About twelve miles round trip
Elevation: 3,040-5,446 feet
Maps: Big Bend National Park topo map, Big Bend National Park "Trails Illustrated" topo map, Twin Peaks and Bone Spring 7.5-minute USGS quads
Best season: October through March
Water availability: Alamo and Lost Springs; see text
Special attractions: Views, solitude
Finding the trailhead: From park headquarters at Panther Junction, drive north toward Marathon about 22.7 miles to the dirt road turnoff on the left (or drive 4.2 miles south from the Persimmon Gap visitor center on the same park road). The junction is marked with signs for Terlingua Ranch and other destinations. The road is a county road, but its condition varies tremendously. During and after the rainy season are usually the worst times to visit. Mud and washouts can make the road virtually impassable to any vehicle. Sand is usually the problem the rest of the year. Experienced drivers can sometimes make the drive with a sedan, but a high clearance vehicle or four-wheel-drive is probably a better bet. Use great care crossing the long sandy stretches. Check with park rangers about the road's condition before attempting it. Follow the main county road about 14.2 miles to an old road forking off to the left. The old road, which looks more like a dry wash, is now closed and marked with a "Road Closed" sign. If you miss the old road, keep driving until you hit the well-marked fenced and signed park boundary at about 15.1 miles. Turn around and carefully retrace your route a bit less than one mile to the old road. Park at the turnoff.

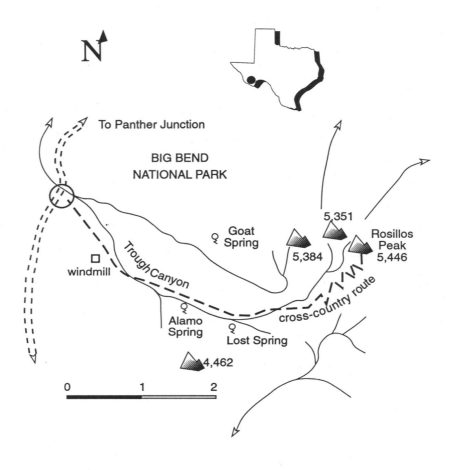

The hike: The Rosillos Mountains were recently given to the National Park Service by the Nature Conservancy. Houston and Ed Harte of San Antonio donated the 67,000-acre ranch to the Conservancy in 1984. At the time, it was the Conservancy's largest preserve in the United States.

The mountains were formed by a large granite laccolith. Although the mountains are not high in an absolute sense, they do rise an impressive 2,600 feet about the surrounding desert. A few small springs lie tucked away in hidden canyons, providing water for wildlife in the otherwise dry and desolate mountain range.

The hike to the summit of Rosillos Peak should be attempted only by fit, experienced hikers in the cooler part of the year. At least one member of the party must be good at route-finding. There is no trail; the route follows rocky canyon bottoms and steep, cactus-covered slopes. Heavy boots, long pants, the USGS quads, a compass, and lots of water are necessities for this hike. The "Trails Illustrated" map is not adequate and in fact contains some errors in the Rosillos Mountains. Although heat is usually the problem at Big Bend, occasional winter storms can bring frigid temperatures to the bare mountains.

Follow the old road southeast toward the mountains. An old windmill will be passed at the mouth of Trough Canyon. After the old road ends, follow the wash up into the canyon. Alamo Spring will be encountered in the canyon bottom a short distance up canyon. Lost Spring lies in the bottom where the canyon forks. The main fork turns left, to the northeast. Do not depend on water from the springs without checking with the Park Service ahead of time.

The park boundary lies on the ridge above Trough Canyon on the south side. Do not cross the fenced and marked boundary; the land on the other side is private.

After you turn northeast in the main canyon fork, begin to climb up the right, or east, wall of the canyon to the ridge top. Follow the ridge top to the northeast, keeping Trough Canyon down below to your left. The ridge steepens as you climb toward the summit. Be sure to stay within the park boundary fence. Finally, the grade moderates as you reach a summit below the main peak. A short walk across an easy saddle to the north-northeast will bring you to the main summit.

Surprisingly, the top of the mountain is quite grassy, with even a few hardy junipers here and there. Views stretch for miles, from the Big Bend country of Texas far into Mexico. Few signs of man are visible, other than a road or two.

The park doesn't allow backcountry camping in the Rosillos Mountains, so plan on a long day. In winter, probably the best time for the hike, the days are short. Get an early start; you will probably need every bit of daylight there is for the entire round trip hike.

If you make it to the summit, be proud; very few others have. Return via the same route, or using the maps and compass, pick an alternate descent back to the trailhead.

HIKE 12: *RANCHERÍAS CANYON*

General description: A moderate day hike through a rugged desert canyon of the Bofecillos Mountains
General location: About twenty miles west of Lajitas
Length: About ten miles round trip
Elevation: 2,500 to 3,360 feet
Maps: Big Bend Ranch State Natural Area Backcountry and River Guide, Redford SE and Agua Adentro 7.5-minute USGS quads
Best season: Fall through spring
Water availability: Unreliable; see text
Special attractions: Rugged desert canyon, solitude
Permit: Required for camping

Rancherías Canyon cuts deep into the Bofecillos Mountains.

Finding the trailhead: From Lajitas, drive west on FM 170 about 22.2 miles to the well-marked West Rancherías Trailhead on the right.

The hike: Big Bend Ranch, with over 200,000 acres, is an enormous area of land recently purchased by the state and managed as a natural area by the Texas Parks and Wildlife Department. The desert park extends from the craggy heights of the Bofecillos Mountains down to the deep canyons of the Rio Grande on the Mexican border. FM 170 crosses the southern edge of Big Bend Ranch along the river. The route, possibly the most scenic drive in Texas, traverses a twisted and tortured landscape of ancient lava flows and water-cut canyons.

Big Bend Ranch is largely undeveloped. This hike, although generally easy to follow, has not been improved and is basically a cross-country route. The hike follows a canyon into the heart of the Bofecillos Mountains on relatively easy terrain. Hikers with some experience should have little trouble following the route. Don't let the bleak appearance of the terrain at the trailhead discourage you. Rancherías Canyon is a hidden jewel, unknown to most people.

The trail starts at the right side of the parking area. The path, marked with rock cairns, drops immediately into a small desert wash. It follows the sandy bottom of the wash, paralleling the highway, a short distance before climbing

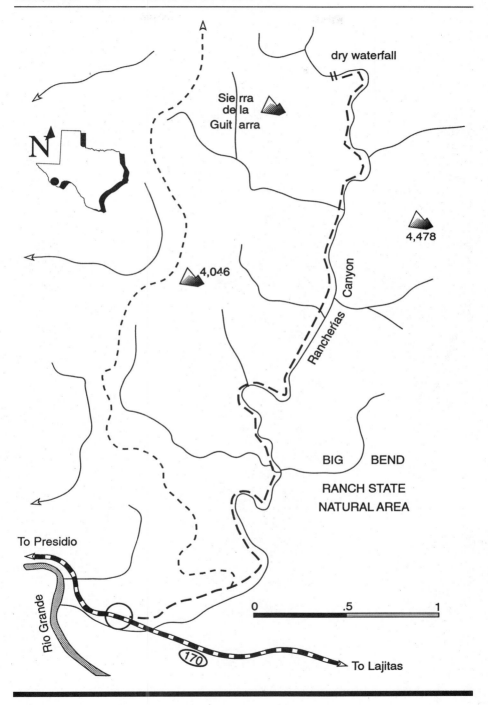

out onto an old unused four-wheel-drive road. Turn left onto the old road and follow it up toward the mountains away from the highway. After about .5 mile, the road forks at some large rock cairns. Take the right fork and drop down into the canyon. The left fork is part of the large Rancherías Loop Trail. The old road ends at the canyon bottom.

The rest of the hike is easy to follow. Just walk up the main canyon into the mountains. Depending on rainfall, parts of the canyon will have a small flowing stream. At about two miles, the trail enters the spectacular high-walled part of the canyon. Old lava flows from the Bofecillos and Sierra Rica volcanos form the sheer walls. Cliffs and occasional cottonwoods, willows, and tamarisks provide shady rest areas on hot afternoons. The canyon climbs at a gradual, easy grade all the way to the end of the hike. Although the route is not an improved trail, much of it follows a smooth sand and gravel surface. Occasional rocky areas slow the pace down some.

The hike ends after a narrow sheer-walled bend in the canyon at seventy-five-foot high Rancherías Falls. Cliffs make it dangerous to climb around the pour-off, so I recommend that you don't try. If you do the hike after a good late-summer rainy

The spectacular narrow slot of Closed Canyon should not be entered if rain is possible.

season, you may be lucky enough to see the pour-off with a flowing waterfall. Return to the trailhead by the same route. If you miss the old road, don't worry. The canyon crosses the highway just east of the trailhead.

This can be an extremely hot hike from April to October. It's not uncommon for summer temperatures to reach 110 degrees along the river in summer. Try to hike during cooler parts of the year. The water in the canyon is not reliable, so plan to carry plenty for this long a trip. Most of the hike follows the canyon bottom, so watch the weather. Flash floods can roar down from the mountains above. Don't leave anything of value (or ideally anything at all) in your car. You may wish to arrange a car shuttle with one of the outfitters in Lajitas or Terlingua, especially for an extended trip, if you don't want to leave your car unattended.

If you like this hike, consider trying the much longer Rancherías Loop Trail. The loop circles deep into the rugged back country of the Bofecillos Mountains, traversing rugged canyons and passing springs and historic sites. The hike usually requires two to three days to complete.

HIKE 13: *CLOSED CANYON*

General description: An easy day hike into a slot canyon
General location: About twenty miles west of Lajitas
Length: About 1.5 miles round trip
Elevation: 2,700-2,600 feet
Maps: Big Bend Ranch State Natural Area Backcountry and River Guide, Redford SE 7.5-minute USGS quad
Best season: All year
Water availability: None
Special attractions: Very narrow 200-foot deep gorge
Finding the trailhead: From Lajitas, drive west about twenty-one miles along FM 170, the River Road, into Big Bend Ranch State Natural Area. The highway is one of the most scenic in Texas. The well-marked trailhead is on the left, or south, side of the highway.

The hike: Big Bend Ranch State Natural Area was recently acquired by the state from private interests. The huge area adjoins Big Bend National Park and contains about 250,000 acres of rugged desert terrain fronting Colorado Canyon of the Rio Grande. Two trails have been developed in the park, this one and Hike #12, the Rancherías Trail. Many more hikes should develop as the park becomes established.

Closed Canyon is a short canyon that drains the valley surrounding the trailhead. Through the eons, water has cut a narrow gorge to the Rio Grande through a mesa composed of welded volcanic tuff. Because the tuff is very erosion resistant and homogenous, the canyon became very deep and narrow, forming a slot. Although common in sandstone areas such as southern Utah, such slot canyons are rare in Texas.

The trail drops down into a wash by following an old road bed. The wash

HIKE 13 CLOSED CANYON

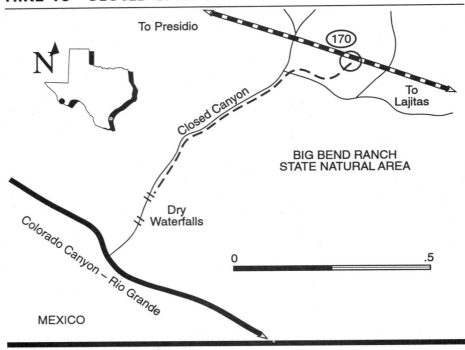

leads very quickly into the obvious yawning mouth of the canyon. The trail follows the dry canyon bottom, alternating between a gravel surface and polished rock. Although the canyon winds some, overall it trends south-southwest. After about a half mile, the canyon bottom starts to have small drops of several feet. Initially, the dry waterfalls, or pour-offs, are easy to climb down, but they get larger as you progress. Make sure that you can climb back up before you jump down; the polished rock lacks handholds and can be slick. Occasionally rain water will be pooled at the base of some of the pour-offs, necessitating wading.

At about .75 mile, you will hit a ten foot pour-off. It's easy to get down, but difficult to climb back up. Good climbers can get back up on the right side, but most people should stop here. A short distance further, the canyon drops about twenty feet in two stages. The tantalizing sound of the rushing waters of the Rio Grande echoes up from around the bend, but only expert rock climbers with some sort of fixed rope should attempt the drop. Just beyond, the canyon drops again, this time much more. The river will be in sight, but ropes and rappelling and ascending equipment are necessary to proceed further.

Except for the pour-offs at the end, this is a fun easy hike any time of year. Even on scorching summer days, the high canyon walls shade much of the canyon. Watch the weather, especially in the late summer rainy season. The sheer walls don't offer many escape routes if a flash flood roars through.

HIKE 14: *GUADALUPE PEAK*

General description: A strenuous day hike or overnight trip to the highest point in Texas

General location: Guadalupe Mountains National Park

Length: About 8.5 or ten miles round trip

Elevation: 5,820-8,749 feet

Maps: Guadalupe Mountains National Park "Trails Illustrated" topo map, National Park Service brochure, Guadalupe Peak 7.5-minute USGS quad

Best season: All year

Water availability: Trailhead

Special attractions: Views, rugged mountains

Permit: Required for camping

Finding the trailhead: From the new visitor center just off of US 62-180, drive up the paved road to the Pine Springs Campground, about .5 mile northwest. Park in front of the large trailhead sign at the far side of the RV area.

The hike: Anyone who thinks that Texas is flat needs to be taken on this hike. Guadalupe Peak, the highest point in Texas and the Guadalupe Mountains, towers a vertical mile above the salt flats to the west. Cliffs flanking the west side of the mountains are over 1500 feet high. El Capitan Peak, just to the south, rises out of the desert like the prow of an enormous ship and forms probably the most notable natural landmark in Texas.

The Guadalupe Mountains and Big Bend form the two premier hiking areas in Texas. The Guadalupe Mountains are a large wedge-shaped mountain range that rises in New Mexico, with the point of the wedge lying in Texas. Although the bulk of the range lies in New Mexico, the highest and much of the most spectacular parts lie in Texas in Guadalupe Mountains National Park. The range is not especially high by most standards, but its great relief makes it very prominent.

The trail to the summit has one of the biggest climbs in Texas, but is well-built with a steady moderate grade. Be sure to stock up on water at the campground; there is none along the way. The well-marked trail starts at the large trailhead sign. It forks in about 100 feet; go left toward the peak. The trail forks again in about 100 yards, giving two options for the climb. Ignore the left to El Capitan. The middle fork to the peak is for hikers only and climbs steeply for about .8 miles before rejoining the righthand route. The right fork goes to several destinations, including Guadalupe Peak, and is for both hikers and horses. The right fork rejoins the middle fork in about 1.7 miles, adding .9 miles to the climb. The right fork is less steep and should be considered for the ascent even though it's longer.

The middle fork route is easy to follow. Just climb steeply uphill until you rejoin the horse trail at about .8 miles. The right fork, the horse route, goes about .75 miles further up the canyon before forking again. The right fork continues up the canyon to Devils Hall (See Hike #19). Go left to Guadalupe Peak and begin climbing out of Pine Canyon. At about 1.7 miles you will rejoin the hikers-only

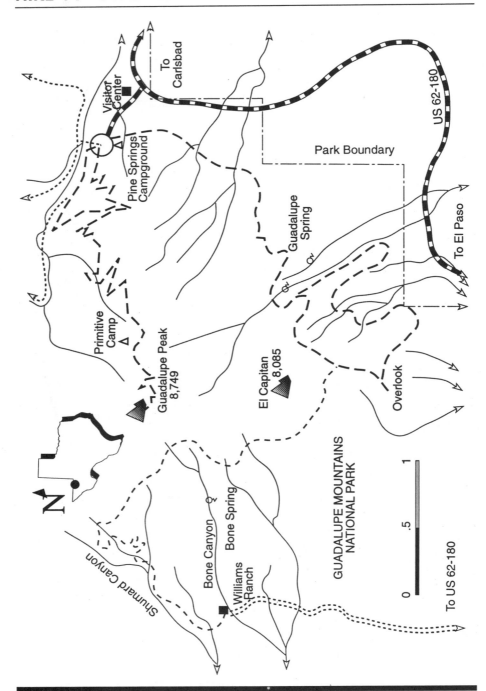

To Carlsbad

Visitor Center

Pine Springs Campground

US 62-180

Park Boundary

Guadalupe Spring

To El Paso

Primitive Camp

Guadalupe Peak 8,749

El Capitan 8,085

Overlook

N

GUADALUPE MOUNTAINS NATIONAL PARK

Bone Canyon

Bone Spring

Williams Ranch

Shumard Canyon

0   .5   1

To US 62-180

A gnarled alligator juniper clings to life below Guadalupe Peak.

route. Stay right and continue to climb. The trail rounds a ridge onto a north-facing slope about .5 miles from the trail junction and switchbacks through ponderosa pines and Douglas firs. At about four miles (via the longer route), you will pass the spur trail to the Guadalupe Peak campsite in a meadow area, about the only halfway level area on the entire climb.

The campsite is spectacular, although as is true with all high country trails in the Guadalupes, you will have to carry all your water. Be wary of camping here in the spring. The site is not very well sheltered and spring winds in the Guadalupes can be something to behold. The Guadalupes are probably the windiest place in Texas with measured winds of over 120 MPH.

From the campsite, the trail drops slightly down a cliff on a wooden footbridge to a partly wooded saddle. From the saddle, the trail resumes switchbacking up the final stretch to the summit, reached at about 5 miles via the longer route. A metal pyramid commemorating the postal service and airlines marks the high point on the bare summit ridge. The west side of the ridge drops off with 1700-foot cliffs, enough to make a bighorn sheep swoon. The views stretch for miles, from the Davis Mountains far to the southeast to Sierra Blanca and the Capitan Mountains far to the north in New Mexico. Never again will you believe that Texas is flat. Unfortunately, even this far from any city, smog often limits the view. Most of the haze comes from unrestricted Mexican industry, El Paso, and the cities of Arizona and southern California.

The hike can be hot in summer, but an early start will make it quite bearable. Spring can be windy, but the temperatures are usually pleasant. Winter is usually a good time to climb, but check weather forecasts. Winter storms can blow in surprisingly suddenly. Although snow usually melts quickly, good quantities can be dumped by occasional storms. Much of the trail is very exposed to lightning, so try to get an early start in late summer.

HIKE 15: *BUSH MOUNTAIN*

General description: A strenuous two-or three-day hike through the Guadalupe Mountains high country
General location: Guadalupe Mountains National Park
Length: About seventeen miles round-trip
Elevation: 5,820-8,631 feet
Maps: Guadalupe Mountains National Park "Trails Illustrated" topo map, National Park Service brochure, Guadalupe Peak and PX Flat 7.5-minute USGS quads
Best season: All year
Water availability: Trailhead
Special attractions: Views, second highest peak in Texas, forested high country
Permit: Required for camping
Finding the trailhead: Follow the same directions as those for Hike #14.

The hike: This hike follows a loop through some of the most scenic high country in Texas. Endless views are interspersed with dense forests of pine and fir. The

The Guadalupe Mountains rise almost a vertical mile above the desert floor.

longest stretch of trail in Texas above 8,000 feet lies along this route.

As with all high country hikes in the Guadalupes, lack of water is a problem. Plan to carry all that you need. The trail starts from the Pine Springs Campground, and hits two junctions very soon after starting. Follow the signs for the Tejas Trail. Go right at the first junction and left at the second.

The trail climbs slowly up the wall of Pine Spring Canyon at a steady but generally moderate grade. As with most Guadalupe trails, it tends to be rocky, even though relatively well maintained. The four mile climb to the crest is on the unshaded south-facing slope of the canyon—it tends to be hot most of the year. Try to get a very early start.

Take a break and get your heart rate down when you finally top out. The worst of the climb is over. The mountaintops to the north are clad with scattered groves of ponderosa and limber pine, Douglas fir, and alligator juniper in sharp contrast to the desert slopes that you just climbed.

The trail forks three ways at the crest. Go left, off of the Tejas Trail, toward Bush Mountain. The trail follows the north rim of Pine Spring Canyon to the summit of Bush Mountain, the second-highest peak in Texas. The ups and downs along the way get a little tiring, but aren't nearly as bad as the climb up out of Pine Spring Canyon.

Unlike most of the other peaks in the Guadalupes, Bush Mountain has a large, relatively flat, partly wooded summit. Views to the west, down the sheer western escarpment, are spectacular, with a drop of almost one vertical mile. To the south, topping the abrupt escarpment, loom Bartlett, Shumard, and Guadalupe peaks, the other three of the four highest peaks in Texas. Many years

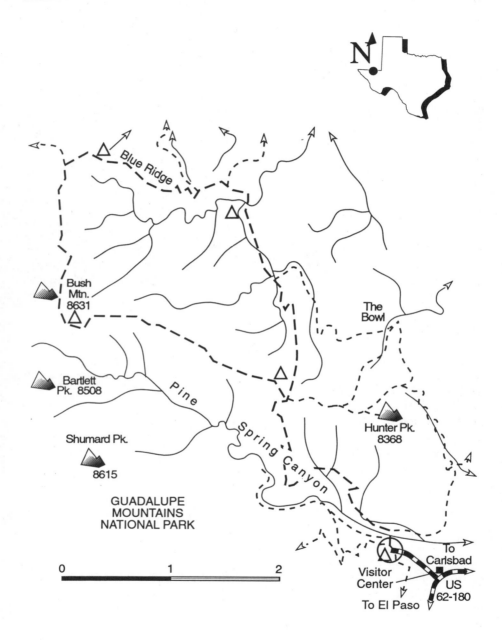

Blue Ridge

Bush
Mtn.
8631

The
Bowl

Bartlett
Pk. 8508

Pine

Spring Canyon

Hunter Pk.
8368

Shumard Pk.

8615

GUADALUPE
MOUNTAINS
NATIONAL PARK

0   1   2

To
Carlsbad

Visitor
Center   US
62-180

To El Paso

ago, in a fit of adolescent frenzy, I climbed all four peaks in one day. With no trail and many thousands of feet of elevation gain and loss, I recommend it only to masochists.

The trail continues north along the western escarpment for about two miles to a junction. Be sure to watch the sunset from somewhere along here if you camp at the Bush Mountain or Blue Ridge campsites. At the junction, go right, east, away from the escarpment. If you have time and enough water, you can enlarge the loop by going left; this route will take you into some of the least-visited areas of the park.

After the fork the trail follows Blue Ridge for over a mile before dropping down to the Marcus Trail junction. Stay right, toward the Tejas Trail. In about .3 mile, the trail hits the Tejas Trail. Go right, back toward Pine Springs Campground. The trail drops into a lushly-wooded canyon and gradually follows it upstream. Ignore the left fork to the Bowl about a mile up the canyon. After about 2.5 miles, the trail hits the junction at the start of the loop. From there, just follow the same trail back down into Pine Spring Canyon to the campground. For variety, the hike can be combined with part of Hike #21, the Bowl.

The high country is very pleasant in summer, although the climb out of Pine Spring Canyon will be hot. Spring has notorious winds at times. Winter is generally good, but check weather forecasts. The Guadalupes are high enough to get a few winter storms and even heavy snow on occasion. Snow usually melts off quickly, however. Fall is probably my favorite time in the Guadalupes. You'll have the high country almost to yourself, while the crowds jam McKittrick Canyon. Maples grow along the route, especially on the return leg of the loop in the wooded canyon bottom. Even a few aspens survive in the high country if you know where to look.

HIKE 16: LOST PEAK

General description: A moderate day hike to the summit of a remote Guadalupe Mountains peak
General location: Guadalupe Mountains National Park
Length: About 6.5 miles round trip
Elevation: 6,290-7,830 feet
Maps: Guadalupe Mountains National Park "Trails Illustrated" topo map, Guadalupe Peak 7.5-minute USGS quad
Best season: All year
Water availability: Trailhead, Dog Spring; see text
Special attractions: Views, fall maples
Permit: Required for camping
Finding the trailhead: The trailhead is most easily approached from New Mexico. Drive about twelve miles northwest of Carlsbad on US 285 to the NM 137 junction. Turn left   (southwest) and follow paved NM 137 up into the mountains. At about forty-five miles, the road drops abruptly down to the big valley of Dog Canyon. In the bottom of the valley, the road forks after passing through the short canyon known as El Paso Gap. Go left, following signs to the

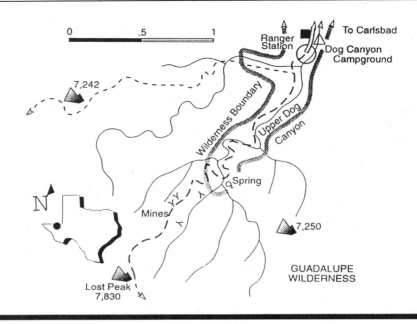

national park. At about six miles, the road crosses into Texas and the park. Just beyond, at the end of the road, lie the Dog Canyon ranger station, campground, and trailhead. A long, dusty alternate route is possible by coming via Dell City, Texas.

The hike: Guadalupe Mountains National Park does not receive heavy tourist traffic, but, because of its remote location, Dog Canyon receives much less visitation than the rest of the park. The large valley of Dog Canyon narrows abruptly at the state line and forms a well-defined canyon at the trailhead. Although still steep-walled, the canyon does not have the towering cliffs of the eastern canyons such as McKittrick and Pine Spring.

Alligator junipers shade the small, grassy, developed campground at the trailhead, creating a beautiful place to spend the night before or after your hike. The Bush Mountain Trail forks to the right just after the start. Stay left on the Tejas Trail and continue up the main canyon through patchy woods of juniper, pinyon pine, velvet ash, bigtooth maple, and scattered ponderosa pine. The maples turn brilliant gold and scarlet in the fall. Dog Canyon is a good place to see the color without fighting the crowds at McKittrick Canyon.

At roughly 1.5 miles, the trail leaves the canyon bottom and begins climbing in earnest. Dog Spring lies just up the canyon from where the trail begins its climb out. Check at the ranger station about its status before depending on it. Since the spring is so close to the trailhead, it's probably easier to fill up at the start and not have to worry about purification.

The trail passes a ruined miner's cabin on the right part way up the ridge. Scattered on the ridge above the cabin lie several small copper mines. The long-abandoned mines were unsuccessful, not surprising in the poorly mineralized Guadalupes. Don't try to enter the hazardous tunnels or disturb any of the ruins.

The last part of the hike is a long steady climb up the ridgetop to the peak. The trail passes through scattered patches of stunted ponderosa pine and Douglas fir. The summit is just off the trail to the right, when you reach the rim of West Dog Canyon. The spectacular view stretches from the tallest peaks of the Guadalupes to the south, to the much higher Sacramento and Capitan mountains far to the north in New Mexico.

The Tejas Trail continues far into the Guadalupe high country and can be easily extended to connect with Hike #15, Bush Mountain, and Hike #21, the Bowl. A beautiful fifteen-mile loop, probably the least traveled in the park, can be followed by continuing along the Tejas Trail, turning right on the Blue Ridge Trail, turning right again on the Bush Mountain Trail, and following it back to the fork at the trailhead. If a car shuttle or ride can be obtained, the full length of the Tejas Trail, from Dog Canyon to Pine Springs makes a classic twelve-mile day hike or backpack.

If you camp on this hike, you must continue another 1.5 miles to the Mescalero campsite. Be sure to pick up a permit ahead of time. As with all high country hikes in the Guadalupes, there are no water sources, so you must carry all that you need. You are very unlikely to see the few black bears in the mountains, but take proper precautions anyway. The upper part of the hike is exposed to lightning, especially on late summer afternoons. Check weather forecasts in winter before you hike. Snowstorms aren't common, but can be sudden and powerful.

HIKE 17: McKITTRICK CANYON

General description: An easy day hike into McKittrick Canyon, famous for its fall color
General location: Guadalupe Mountains National Park
Length: About seven miles round trip
Elevation: 4,980-5,320 feet
Maps: Guadalupe Mountains National Park "Trails Illustrated" topo map, National Park brochure, Guadalupe Peak and Independence Spring 7.5-minute USGS quads
Best season: All year
Water availability: Trailhead, McKittrick Creek
Special attractions: Maples in fall, permanent stream, rugged canyon
Finding the trailhead: From the main park visitor center, drive northeast toward Carlsbad on US 62-180 for about eight miles to the marked McKittrick Canyon junction. Turn left toward the mountains on the paved road and follow it about four miles to the end at the McKittrick Canyon visitor center.

The hike: McKittrick Canyon is one of the most famous scenic spots in Texas. The canyon mouth conceals its secrets well. The dry desert slopes give little sign of the lush vegetation and rushing stream found hidden in the canyon. McKittrick is particularly famous for its large stands of bigtooth maples. In the fall, some parts of the canyon resemble New England more than West Texas. If you do come in autumn, try to avoid the weekends because heavy crowds descend on the canyon during fall color. In fact, the park has begun limiting the number of people allowed in the canyon on fall weekends. Because the canyon is very delicate and so many people visit, be sure to stay on the trail to avoid trampling the vegetation.

During the rest of the year, the canyon is relatively quiet. The trail starts on the other side of the visitor center. Be sure to sign the register. Ignore the nature trail loop on the left and the Permian Reef Geology Trail on the right and continue straight ahead into the canyon. The trail quickly drops into the canyon and crosses to the other side of the wash. The trail follows what used to be a road up to Wallace Pratt's old lodge. It follows the benches above the wash and makes occasional crossings. The third crossing contains a surprise. Except in very dry times, a stream flows down canyon at that crossing.

The stream is the only place in Texas with a reproducing population of trout. Scientists are unsure whether the trout are native, stocked, or a cross between the two. Because of the small population, fishing isn't allowed. On hot days, resist the temptation to wade in the stream. With the heavy visitation, waders would quickly pollute the stream. If you drink the water, be sure to purify it first.

The permanent stream in McKittrick Canyon hosts the only reproducing tront population in Texas.

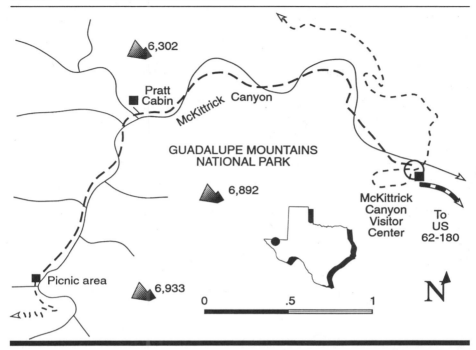

The next stream crossing is also wet, but the rest of the crossings to the Pratt house are dry. Apparently the deep gravels in that part of the canyon absorb the stream's flow. At about 2.3 miles, at a large canyon junction, you will encounter a picnic area and a trail junction. The right fork goes only 200 feet or so up to the Pratt house, well hidden in the woods. The house is interesting; it is made almost entirely of stone, even the roof. A park ranger is often stationed there. A bathroom is attached to the garage and water is sometimes available (check before you start your hike).

The trail continues up the south fork of the canyon from the picnic area. The stream reappears soon. Much of the trail passes through woods consisting of ponderosa pine, alligator juniper, oaks, ash, and large stands of maples. At a little over three miles, the trail forks. The right fork begins to climb up out of the canyon to the canyon rim. Go left to the Grotto picnic area. At about 3.4 miles the trail comes into the picnic area, a shaded site tucked up against a cliff with several small caves. Just a bit further up the canyon, the trail ends at the old stone line camp. Please don't disturb the old building.

Because of its delicate nature, the canyon beyond the line camp is closed to visitation. To extend your hike, take the right fork at the junction just before the Grotto picnic area. It climbs up out of the canyon into the high country. The trail can be followed all the way to the Bowl (See Hike #21), Bush Mountain (See Hike #15), Lost Peak (See Hike #16), or other destinations. To camp at McKittrick you must climb up to the designated sites in the high country. No camping is allowed in the canyon itself.

Be sure to note the times that the gate is open at the McKittrick turnoff on US 62-180. Unless you have obtained a camping permit for the high country, you must leave the canyon in time to reach the gate by closing time.

HIKE 18: *EL CAPITAN*

General description: A moderate day hike to overlooks below the sheer cliffs of El Capitan Peak
General location: Guadalupe Mountains National Park
Length: About eleven miles round trip
Elevation: 5,400-6,360 feet
Maps: Guadalupe Mountains National Park "Trails Illustrated" topo map, National Park Service brochure, Guadalupe Peak and Guadalupe Pass 7.5-minute USGS quads
Best season: Fall through spring
Water availability: Trailhead, Guadalupe Spring
Special attractions: Views
Finding the trailhead: Follow the same directions as those for Hike #14, Guadalupe Peak.

The hike: El Capitan rises above the Chihuahuan Desert like the prow of some enormous ship. The towering cliffs are an exposure of the massive fossilized Capitan Reef that lies under much of West Texas. Faults raised the Guadalupe Mountains up as high as 5,000 feet above the surrounding desert. The distinctive shape of El Capitan forms one of the most notable landmarks in the Southwest. This hike follows a loop trail to viewpoints below the peak.

Like many of the Guadalupe trails, this one starts at the Pine Springs Campground. Some old maps show the trail as starting from a corral along US 62-180 just south of the visitor center, but the trailhead has been changed to the campground.

The trail starts from the RV parking area in the campground. After 100 feet or so, the trail forks. Go left toward El Capitan and Guadalupe Peak. After another 100 yards, the trail forks again. Go left toward El Capitan.

The trail winds along the base of the mountains through thick grasses and an occasional juniper. After about 2.5 miles, the trail climbs several hundred feet over a rounded ridge extending east from the main mountain mass. It then descends down into Guadalupe Canyon and forks after crossing a rocky wash. If you need water, Guadalupe Spring lies in a parallel drainage just east of the trail junction. It's not obvious; look for green grass and vegetation. Purify any water taken. Be sure to take a break under one of the trees scattered along the canyon bottom. The rest of the hike has little shade.

The marked junction is the start of the loop. I chose to go right to get the climbing over with first. The trail climbs about 500 feet up the steep slopes below the cliffs of El Capitan Peak. About a mile from Guadalupe Canyon, the trail

An early winter storm frosts trees in Pine Spring Canyon.

forks again. The right fork continues another 5.1 miles to Williams Ranch on the empty west side of the park. Go left to the Salt Basin Overlook and the rest of the loop. The overlook gives tremendous views of the Salt Flats and distant Cornudas Mountains and Sierra Diablo.

As you continue around the loop, you will notice that a long finger of the loop extends south along a ridge top. If you're good at reading a topo map and doing cross-country travel, you can cut across the ridge and save a mile. From the end of the loop, follow the same trail from Guadalupe Canyon back to the campground.

The trail has little shade, except near the start and in Guadalupe Canyon, so I don't recommend it in summer. The trail is one of the least used in the park, so it's good for escaping the crowds. If you have time and energy, be sure to follow the trail all the way to historic Williams Ranch. The route contours along the slopes below the awesome western escarpment of the Guadalupes before dropping down to the weathered clapboard ranch house lost in the desert slopes below Bone Canyon. With an off-trail detour, water can be obtained at Bone Spring, the only significant source of water on the entire west side. To go to Williams Ranch will probably require an overnight trip or, better yet, a car shuttle to Williams Ranch. Park permission and either a four wheel drive or high clearance vehicle is necessary to reach the ranch.

HIKE 19: *DEVILS HALL*

General description: An easy day hike to a narrow gorge cut by Pine Spring Canyon
General location: Guadalupe Mountains National Park
Length: About 4.2 miles round trip
Elevation: 5,820-6,360 feet
Maps: Guadalupe Mountains National Park "Trails Illustrated" topo map, National Park Service brochure, Guadalupe Peak 7.5-minute USGS quad
Best season: All year
Water availability: Trailhead
Special attractions: Rugged canyon, maples
Finding the trailhead: Follow the same directions as Hike 14, Guadalupe Peak.

The hike: Most of the major canyons of the Guadalupe Mountains drain to the east. Pine Spring Canyon, one of the largest canyons in the park, is no exception. The trailhead lies in the broad mouth of the canyon below a rim as much as 2,500 feet high. The four highest peaks in Texas circle the Pine Spring Canyon drainage. The dry canyon quickly narrows as you follow it upstream. Devils Hall is a short narrow slot as little as fifteen feet wide that has been cut by the canyon.

The trailhead is marked by a large sign at the far end of the RV area in the campground. Be sure to sign in on the register. The trail follows the main canyon for the entire route. Follow the signs to Devils Hall. Go left at the first junction in 100 feet or so. At the second junction after another 100 yards, go right, following the trail to Devils Hall and the horse route up Guadalupe Peak. In about .5 mile or so, the horse trail to Guadalupe Peak goes left. Stay right, to Devils Hall.

The Devils Hall Trail drops into the canyon bottom and follows the rocky wash for the remainder of the hike. No actual trail exists. Unless a recent flood has washed them away, rock cairns mark the route. Even without markers, just follow the main canyon bottom up; it's virtually impossible to get lost. The route is somewhat rocky for walking, but not too difficult.

As the canyon bends to the left, or southwest, it becomes narrower and more wooded. Ponderosa pine, bigtooth maple, and velvet ash are more common. The maples and ashes in Pine Spring Canyon can be almost as spectacular as McKittrick Canyon, but the trail will have only a small fraction of the people on fall color days. Soon the trail makes a big horseshoe bend to the northeast.

The canyon turns again, to the northwest, at a narrow point in the canyon. The narrow point, sometimes called the Devils Gate, is marked unmistakably by towering columns of limestone on each side of the wash. The wash pinches down to a narrow slot, with stairstep-like rock layers forming the canyon bottom. About .25 mile past the gates, the canyon again pinches down, this time at the Devils Hall. The hall is a deep, narrow cut through multilayered limestone.

Although Pine Spring Canyon is usually dry, flash floods roar down the canyon on occasion, especially during the rainy season of late summer. Don't get caught in either the Devils Gate or the Devils Hall in heavy rains. The canyon beyond the hall is somewhat rough and rocky but rewarding for hikers. Eventually, the canyon tops out on the high western crest of the mountains.

HIKE 20: *SMITH SPRING*

General description: An easy day hike to a small oasis
General location: Guadalupe Mountains National Park
Length: About 2.3 miles round trip
Elevation: 5,530-5,900 feet
Maps: Guadalupe Mountains National Park "Trails Illustrated" topo map, National Park brochure, Guadalupe Peak 7.5-minute USGS quad
Best season: All year
Water availability: Smith Spring
Special attractions: Lush riparian area at spring, maples
Finding the trailhead: From the visitor center, drive northeast on US 62-180 about 1.5 miles toward Carlsbad. Turn left on the gravel road to Frijole Ranch. After .75 mile, park at the old ranch at the end of the road.

The hike: The hike starts at the old Frijole Ranch. Part of the ranch house is considered to be the oldest substantial building in the area. The Rader brothers settled here in the 1870s, at the permanent spring. The Smith family moved here in 1906 and made most of their living from truck farming and a small orchard. To get their produce to market, they would drive their wagon all night when it was cool to Van Horn, over sixty miles away. Their ranch became the center of the local ranching community, with a post office from 1912 to 1940. The ranch name came from the locals' abundant diet of beans, or frijoles. Smith Spring and Manzanita Spring, along this hike, were important sources of water to both wildlife and livestock during the area's ranching days.

Before you start the hike, walk around the old ranch. Under the tall oaks, the spring still flows strongly from the spring house. The large trail head sign is on the west side of the ranch parking lot. Be sure to register. The trail is a loop that can be done either way. I prefer to take it in a counter-clockwise direction.

From the sign, following the old, closed road past the ranch buildings to Manzanita Spring. The first part of the trail is almost level. At about .3 mile, the trail reaches the large pond formed by Manzanita Spring. The spring was the site of a large battle between the US Army and the Apaches. The army made a surprise attack and destroyed most of the Indians' winter stores. An interpretive sign at the spring describes the attack in detail.

From the spring, the trail begins a gradual climb toward the base of the mountains. Without grazing, the grasses on the mountain slopes are recovering well. Pinyon pines and junipers are returning too. The trail crosses a dry wash and begins climbing more steeply. Suddenly, at about 1.2 miles, the trail drops down to the spring, a surprisingly lush oasis of ponderosa pine, Texas madrone, and bigtooth maple. A small stream rushes down the canyon bottom, making

HIKE 19   DEVILS HALL   HIKE 20   SMITH SPRING
HIKE 21   THE BOWL

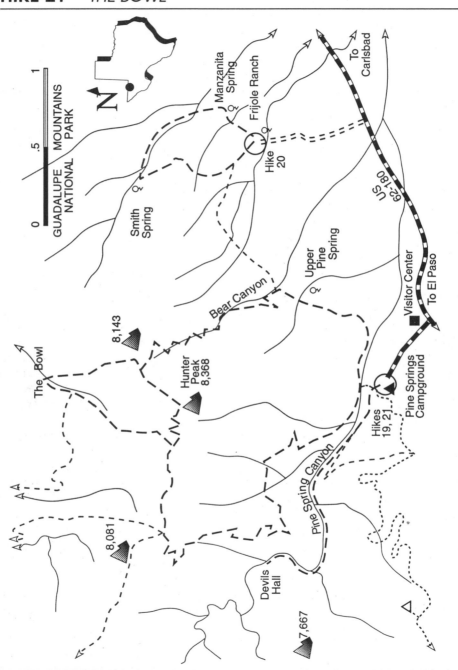

62

a welcome sound on a hot summer day. Be sure to stay on the trail; the small area's vegetation could be easily trampled. If necessary, water can be obtained from the spring (and purified), but on this short a hike it's better to carry what you need. Because the area is small and delicate, the Park Service does not allow camping.

From the spring, the trail drops back down toward the valley. A little before reaching the ranch, the trail forks. Go left, for the last .25 mile to the trailhead. A sign at the fork is confusing, showing Frijole back the way you came.

HIKE 21: *THE BOWL*

General description: A strenuous day hike or overnight trip to the thickest forest in the Guadalupe Mountains
General location: Guadalupe Mountains National Park
Length: About ten miles round trip
Elevation: 5,820-8,368 feet
Maps: Guadalupe Mountains National Park "Trails Illustrated" topo map, Guadalupe Peak 7.5-minute USGS quad
Best season: All year
Water availability: Trailhead
Special attractions: Views, dense forest
Permit: Required for camping
Finding the trailhead: Follow the same directions as Hike #14, Guadalupe Peak.

The hike: The Bowl contains the largest fragment of the Guadalupe Mountains' relict forest of ponderosa pine, limber pine, and Douglas fir. The mountains have become hotter and drier since the last ice age, forcing the forest to retreat higher and higher. The forest may still be slowly receding, since the climate now provides barely enough moisture for such trees to survive. Large firs and pines still grow in the gently sloping basin of the Bowl, lying just below 8,000 feet. A fire in 1990 burned some of the lush forest, greatly reducing the fuel load without irreparable harm.

The trail starts at the large sign at the back side of the RV camping area. Follow the signs for the Tejas Trail and the Bowl. Go right at the junction just down the way and follow the Tejas Trail across the broad dry wash of Pine Canyon. The trail forks again on the other side of the wash. The right fork will be the return leg of the loop. Go left, following the Tejas Trail.

The first mile or so of the trail climbs at a fairly easy grade, but the next three miles steepen somewhat as it climbs up the north wall of Pine Spring Canyon. Overall, the rocky trail climbs at a fairly steady, moderate grade. In summer the climb is hot, with little shade on the dry, south-facing slope. Finally, at the canyon rim, you will be relieved to find cool pine forests and an easy trail grade.

The trail splits three ways at the rim. If you plan to camp, the Pine Top campsite is to the left about .25 mile along the Bush Mountain Trail. Be sure to get a permit ahead of time. The Tejas Trail continues straight ahead to the north. Go right toward the Bowl and Hunter Peak. The trail follows the canyon rim east for about .5 mile before forking again. The shortest route to the Bowl goes left, but I recommend going straight for .5 mile, to the top of Hunter Peak. The trail climbs several hundred feet to the summit, with another fork to the left along the way that leads to Bear Canyon and also to the Bowl.

The view from Hunter Peak is one of the best in Texas. If you are camping overnight, be sure to watch the sunset from the summit. Backtrack the last half mile to the first turnoff to the Bowl and follow the path into the lush woods of the Bowl. Part way down the trail you'll hit the edge of the forest fire. Although many trees burned, a surprising number survived. Grasses and other vegetation are already recarpeting the ground although there were heavy topsoil losses in places. If water is in the dirt tank just off the trail, you may be fortunate enough to see some elk, especially early in the morning or late in the evening. In fall, the bull elks bugle, an eerie sound that echoes across the mountain tops.

From the trail junction in the center of the Bowl, go right about .8 mile to the rim of Bear Canyon and another trail junction. The righthand fork is the alternate Bowl route from Hunter Peak. Go left, down Bear Canyon and back to the valley. Take your last whiff of pine-scented air before starting the knee-straining descent down Bear Canyon. The rocky trail drops 2,000 feet in about two miles. Go right at the fork at the bottom and hike about 1.5 miles back to the trailhead.

The loop can be done in reverse, but the climb up Bear Canyon is tough, especially with a backpack. If time allows, be sure to camp a night or two up on top. Many possible side trips or extensions are possible from the basic loop. Unfortunately, as with other high country Guadalupe hikes, there is no reliable water source. Plan to carry all that you need, no easy task for anything more than a two or three day trip.

Be aware of the threat of lightning, especially on late summer afternoons. In spring, winds can blow in the Guadalupes unlike anything else that you have ever seen. Winds have been measured here at over 120 MPH. The mountains get only occasional snowstorms in winter, but check the forecast before you hike and go prepared. A friend and I backpacked up to the Bowl one beautiful sunny January day to be awakened in the morning to 60 MPH north winds, falling temperatures, and dark clouds shrouding the peaks just above us. Did we persevere? Heck no, we retreated down the mountain as fast as our legs (or the wind) could carry us.

HIKE 22: *NORTH MOUNT FRANKLIN*

General description: A strenuous day hike to the highest peak in the Franklin Mountains
General location: Franklin Mountains State Park in El Paso
Length: About eight miles round trip
Elevation: 4,820-7,192 feet
Maps: North Franklin Mountain and Canutillo 7.5-minute USGS quads
Best season: Fall through spring
Water availability: None
Special attractions: Views, rugged mountains

Finding the trailhead: From downtown El Paso, follow I-10 west to the Trans-Mountain Highway, Loop 375, exit on the west side of the city. Follow the Trans-Mountain Highway east toward the mountains for about 3.4 miles to the turnoff on the left into Franklin Mountains State Park. Follow the road into a picnic area for about .9 mile to a small gravel loop of picnic tables on the right and park.

The hike: El Paso surrounds the craggy north-south range of the Franklin Mountains on three sides. The range is not especially large or high, but its 3,400-foot rise above the Rio Grande Valley gives it an impressive profile. Except for cottonwoods, ashes, and hackberries hidden away at a few springs, the mountains are cloaked entirely in Chihuahuan Desert vegetation. Franklin Mountains State Park is relatively new and, with 23,000 acres, the third largest in Texas. Almost the entire range lies within the park, creating a small wilderness surrounded by over a million residents in El Paso and Juarez.

The trail follows a rough dirt road, closed to vehicles, from the picnic loop east toward the mountains. The trail follows the old dirt road all the way to the summit. The road was built, unfortunately, in the 1970s by a developer. His action and other encroaching development were the major stimuli for the creation of the park.

The old road climbs gradually into a small canyon but quickly begins to switchback up the slopes at a moderate grade. About halfway up the peak, the road crests the range at a large pass, Mundys Gap. The road descends a short distance down the other side before hitting a junction. Take the road to the right

Clouds cloak the peaks of the Franklin Mountains.

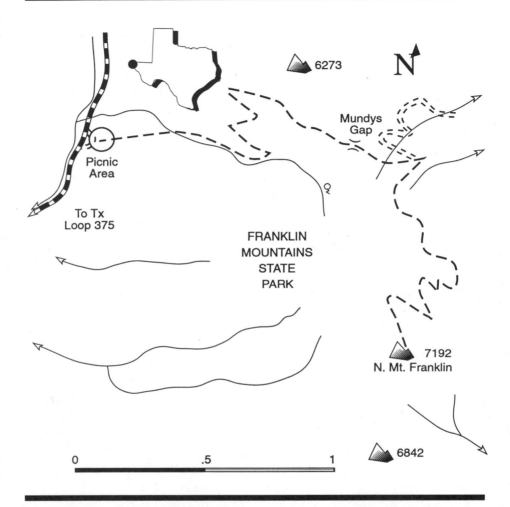

and resume climbing. The road steadily climbs higher, reaching a small saddle partway up. A short side trip to the east from the saddle will take you to Indian Peak, the small peak with an old military building visible on its summit. Continue up a series of switchbacks to reach the summit of North Mount Franklin.

The 360-degree views from the summit are spectacular. El Paso and Juarez stretch in three directions from the foot of the mountains. To the north lie high New Mexico ranges, such as the Organ Mountains, Sierra Blanca, and the Black Range. The Rio Grande forms an emerald ribbon to the west as it flows to the sea.

The peak can be climbed any time of year, but offers little shelter from the sun or any kind of bad weather. If you hike in summer, get a very early start to avoid the heat. In late summer, afternoon thunderstorms can pummel the mountains.

Spring days can be windy. Winter usually provides excellent hiking weather, but occasional snows will fall on the mountains. I was caught just below the summit by a crazy mix of lightning, snow, hail, and rain in early May one year. I quickly discovered that the higher slopes offer little cover.

As of this writing, no good map exists of the trail. The dated USGS map shows only the natural features, not the road used as the route. Check with a ranger before hiking to see if any improved maps have been made.

HIKE 23: ANTHONY'S NOSE

General description: A strenuous cross-country day hike to the summit of the second highest peak in the Franklin Mountains
General location: Franklin Mountains State Park in El Paso
Length: About ten miles round trip
Elevation: 4,600-6,927 feet
Maps: North Franklin Mountain and Canutillo 7.5-minute USGS quads
Best season: Fall through spring
Water availability: None
Special attractions: Views, rugged mountains, solitude
Finding the trailhead: From downtown El Paso, follow I-10 west to the Trans-Mountain Highway (Loop 375) exit on the west side of the city. Follow the Trans-Mountain Highway east toward the mountains for about 3.4 miles to the turnoff on the left into Franklin Mountains State Park. Follow the road into the Tom Mays picnic area for about two miles to the most northerly picnic tables at the end of the paved park road on a hill.

The hike: The Franklin Mountains are a rugged desert mountain range that comprises the jagged spine of the sprawling city of El Paso. The city forms a horseshoe shape around the south end of the range, but the mountains themselves are relatively empty and undisturbed. After a developer began carving roads on the slopes, the state purchased the property for a state park. With over 23,000 acres, the park is one of the largest in Texas and encompasses most of the small range.

The dry mountains are vegetated by Chihuahuan Desert plants such as sotol, lechuguilla, prickly pear, and yucca. One oddity, the large barrel cactus of the Sonoran Desert of Arizona, finds the eastern-most limit of its range in the Franklins. Unfortunately poachers have stolen many of the cacti.

Anthony's Nose is the second highest peak in the Franklins. If you're curious about the peak's name, just look at its profile as you drive by the mountains on I-10 to the west. No developed trail climbs to the summit of Anthony's Nose. The hike is an unmarked rugged cross-country scramble up steep slopes covered with cacti and other spiny plants. Only fit, experienced hikers who are good at map reading and route-finding should attempt the ascent. Sheer cliffs require frequent detours. Not only is the hike long, it ascends 2300 feet. The hike is very hot in summer with little shade. Winter is usually good, but go prepared for the occasional winter storm. Such storms can drop the temperature far below

HIKE 23 ANTHONY'S NOSE

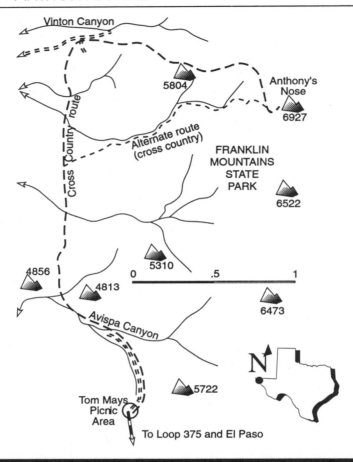

freezing and even dump occasional snows. Get an early start in winter, since the days are short. You will probably need all day for this hike. Hikers need to obtain the relevant topographic maps before doing the climb. The map provided in this guide is not sufficient by itself for this hike.

For the most part, you will have to pick your own route up. My description only covers one possible way to the summit. From the picnic area, drop down into an arm of Avispa Canyon. Follow an old dirt road down into the main part of the canyon. About a mile down the canyon from the start, turn north and climb up out of the canyon between the two hills marked with the elevations "4856" and "4813" on both the topo map and this guidebook's map.

Hike north along the base of the mountains for about 1.5-plus miles until you hit the dirt road that goes up into Vinton Canyon. Along the way you will cross the drainages from two other relatively large, unnamed canyons. Turn right and follow the road a short distance up into Vinton Canyon.

From the end of the road in Vinton Canyon, climb the steep canyon wall to the right (south) to the top of the ridge that radiates out from the main spine of the mountains. By detouring around cliffs and difficult areas, climb the ridge to the east until, grunting and groaning, you reach the crest of the range. Follow the crest south toward the obvious high summit of Anthony's Nose. The north side of the peak drops off in sheer cliffs, so work along the west side of the peak until you can find a safe route to the summit.

The views from the top are tremendous, reaching from high mountains far to the north in New Mexico to mountains far to the south in Mexico. El Paso and Juarez teem with people only a few miles away, but I can guarantee that you will rarely meet anyone on Anthony's Nose. Descend via the same route, picking your way slowly and carefully. Although I have not tried it, I marked one possible alternate route on the map that would shorten the hike somewhat.

Franklin Mountains State Park is relatively new and undeveloped. Improved access to Vinton Canyon and Anthony's Nose may be developed over time, so it would be worthwhile to check with the park staff before your hike. Tom Mays picnic area is open only for day use, so make sure that you get back to your car before they lock the gate at night. Be sure to check on the current hours.

HIKE 24: *HUECO TANKS*

General description: An easy day hike through the jumbled rock masses of Hueco Tanks
General location: About thirty-five miles east of El Paso
Length: About four miles round trip
Elevation: 4,510-4,800 feet
Maps: State park map, Hueco Tanks 7.5-minute USGS quad
Best season: Fall through spring
Water availability: Campground
Special attractions: Rock climbing, pictographs
Finding the trailhead: Drive east of El Paso on US 62-180 for about thirty miles to the turnoff of RM 2775 on the left. Follow RM 2775 north about eight miles to the Hueco Tanks State Historical Park headquarters. The entrance road hits a junction just past the headquarters. Park in the lot across the junction from the entrance road.

The hike: Three large masses of rock form what is known as Hueco Tanks. The igneous rock, a syenite porphyry, intruded into layers of older sedimentary rock. Over time, the limestone eroded away, leaving piles of rock 300 feet high as islands in the desert. The park's name comes from the Spanish word for hollow, referring to the depressions, often water-filled, in the rock.

The park lies in dry Chihuahuan Desert and receives only about eight inches of rain per year. However, the runoff from the bare rock concentrates in hollows, canyons, and cracks in the rocky islands. The coarse igneous soil in these places holds the moisture, allowing trees such as the Arizona oak and the one-seed juniper to grow in the dry climate.

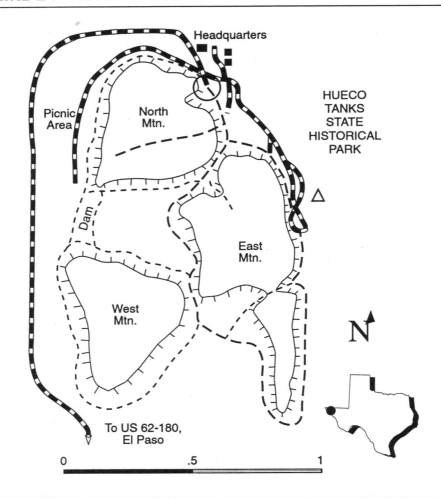

Man first visited Hueco Tanks as far back as 10,000 years ago. Indians continued to utilize the area, probably drawn to the water trapped in the rock depressions. The various groups of people left pictographs scattered throughout the park.

The trail starts at the parking lot at the ruins of the old Butterfield Overland Mail station. Like the Indians, the stage line was attracted by the availability of water. The park is very popular and criss-crossed with both official and unofficial trails. You will need to keep an eye on the map and your location in relation to the three small mountains. Do this, and you are unlikely to get lost.

Hike south, along the east side of North Mountain. Keep an eye on the rock slopes of North Mountain to your right. Head up to the steel railings on the rock when you see them. Follow the marked route as far as it goes and then pick your way through the rocks and cliffs to the summit. Enjoy the view. West Mountain (to the south) is higher, but harder to climb. Give in to temptation and scramble up and down rocks until your muscles ache. Hueco Tanks is a rock climbers' paradise with top climbers from all over the U.S. descending on the park, especially in winter.

Retrace your route back down, or bushwhack a different route. Continue south through the gap between North and East mountains. Look for pictographs on the wall of East Mountain as you hike through the gap. Walk along the side of the East Mountain through the small valley in the middle of the three mountains. Continue south through the gap between East and West mountains and then turn left and loop around the south end of the East Mountain to the campground. Follow the road back north from the campground to the trailhead.

Don't worry about following the route of the suggested hike; it's hard to get lost. You'll probably be tempted to spend the time climbing up and down the rocks of the three mountains. Pictographs are scattered here and there all over the park. Keep a sharp eye out for them, especially in overhangs, caves, and cracks. Don't disturb them or even touch them. They are very old and fragile.

HIKE 25: *FORT DAVIS*

General description: An easy day hike from an historic fort to Davis Mountains State Park
General location: Fort Davis
Length: About four miles round trip
Elevation: 4,880-5,340
Maps: Fort Davis National Historic Site hiking trails brochure, Fort Davis

Fort Davis is one of the best restored frontier forts in the United States.

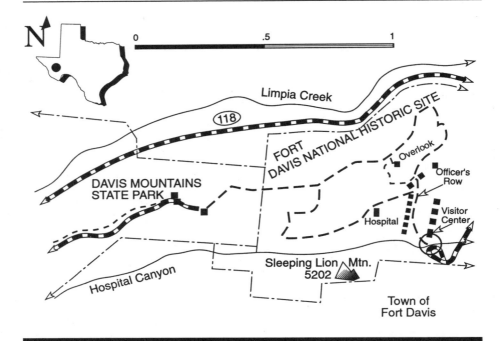

7.5-minute USGS quad
Best season: All year
Water availability: Trailhead
Special attractions: Well-preserved frontier fort, views
Finding the trailhead: The entrance to Fort Davis National Historic Site lies on the north side of the town of Fort Davis. Park at the main visitor center parking lot.

The hike: Fort Davis was founded in 1854 to protect travelers and settlers in West Texas from raiding Comanche and Apache Indians. The fort was occupied by U.S. troops until abandonment in early 1861 because of the Civil War. The Confederates occupied the fort for a year before the fort was abandoned for five years. In 1867, federal troops again were stationed at Fort Davis. A new, much larger fort of stone, adobe, and wood was built over the next twenty years. Fort Davis was one of the first western forts to receive black troops, or "Buffalo Soldiers" as they were known to the Indians. With the surrender of Geronimo in 1886, the Indian wars came to an end. The fort was abandoned in 1891.

More than half of the original fifty structures have been saved. A few have been fully restored. To start the hike, walk across the parade ground to the row of officers' quarters. Be sure to spend some time exploring the old fort. Look for the nature trail sign between the two two-story officers' quarters at the far north end of officers' row. Follow the marked trail up the hill behind the buildings. The trail forks quickly, forming a loop. I prefer the slightly longer right fork. The trail climbs up through interesting rock formations and rejoins the other side of the loop on top of the ridge. The right fork, where the loop joins, is the trail to take. First, however go left a short distance on the other leg of the loop to the overlook. It gives a great view of the fort from above.

The trail continues along the ridgetop toward the state park. A fork goes left down into Hospital Canyon from the main trail. The fork will be the return trail on the way back. Continue west up the ridge. After reaching the high point, the trail continues west and enters the state park. At about two miles the trail reaches a viewpoint and the end of the park road on the ridgetop.

The trail can be followed for another two miles, partway along the road, into the heart of the state park. To return, go back along the same trail to the fork. Turn right and drop down Hospital Canyon to the old hospital and the rest of the fort.

The trail will be hot in summer, especially along the exposed ridgetop, so make an early start. However, the elevation of the mountains is enough to keep the hike bearable even in the peak of summer. The trail is very exposed in thunderstorms.

HIKE 26: *SEMINOLE CANYON*

General description: An easy day hike to the Panther Cave and Amistad Reservoir overlook
General location: About forty-five miles west of Del Rio
Length: About five miles round trip
Elevation: 1,380-1,180 feet
Maps: Seminole Canyon State Historical Park trail map, Seminole Canyon 7.5-minute USGS quad
Best season: Fall through spring
Water availability: None
Special attractions: Large Indian pictographs
Finding the trailhead: From Del Rio, drive west on US 90 about forty-five miles to the Seminole Canyon State Park entrance on the left, or south, side of the highway (or drive about twenty miles east of Langtry). Drive into the park a little over a mile, past the visitor center, to the marked trailhead on the left.

The hike: Seminole Canyon and other nearby canyons are noted for the many pictographs painted in limestone rock shelters. Some are believed to be as old as 8,000 years, making them among the oldest in North America. Some of the impressive panels of rock art are hundreds of feet long. This hike leads to an overlook of Panther Cave and its pictographs.

The trail travels south from the trailhead across gently sloping, basically boring, desert flats to the Rio Grande. At about .6 mile, the trail splits. Take either fork; they rejoin at a little less than 1.5 miles. The right fork is a bit shorter, but the left fork has a nice side trail to an overlook of Seminole Canyon. Several shelters provide shade along the route. You may see mountain bikes using the broad trail.

The trail ends just beyond 2.5 miles at the confluence of the canyon of the Rio Grande and Seminole Canyon. The Rio Grande is dammed at Del Rio, backing the lake up into both canyons. The lake lies 200 feet below the overlook at the base of sheer cliffs. Be careful near the edge. The large rock shelter of Panther Cave lies across the water in Seminole Canyon. Even from across the canyon, the

HIKE 26 *SEMINOLE CANYON*

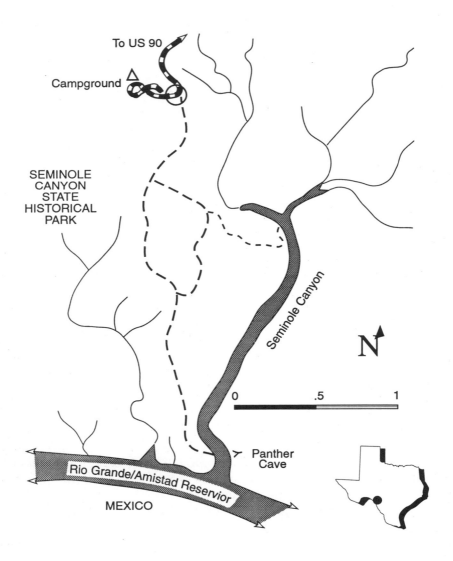

large pictographs, especially the namesake panther, are easily visible. The only way to get closer to the cave is via boat.

If you have time, be sure to take the easy guided hike to Fate Bell Shelter to see some of the pictographs up close.

HIKE 27: *THE LIGHTHOUSE*

General description: An easy day hike to a large shale and sandstone pinnacle
General location: About twenty-five miles southeast of Amarillo
Length: About 6.0 miles round trip
Elevation: 2,830-3,260 feet
Maps: Palo Duro Canyon State Park map, Fortress Cliff 7.5-minute USGS quad
Best season: Fall through spring
Water availability: None
Special attractions: Colorful rock formations
Finding the trailhead: Drive about seventeen miles south of Amarillo on I-27 to the TX 217 exit on the east side of Canyon. Exit and go east, following the Palo Duro Canyon State Park signs. Drive about ten miles east to the entrance of the park. Drive into the park and down into the canyon on the main park road. The road crosses the river several times; the marked trailhead is on the right just after the second crossing.

The Lighthouse rises high above the floor of Palo Duro Canyon.

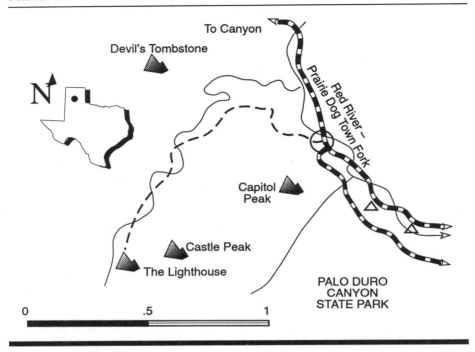

The hike: Most of the high plains of Texas are as flat as a billiard table, so your first view of Palo Duro Canyon will come as a surprise. The flat plains drop abruptly 800 feet to the canyon bottom. Colorful sandstone and shale beds will remind you of the red rock country of Utah. The Prairie Dog Town Fork of the Red River seems tiny compared to the size of the chasm that it has carved.

The popular Lighthouse Trail passes through scenic red and yellow clay badlands and rock formations dotted with Rocky Mountain and one-seed junipers. Except for the last short climb to the base of the Lighthouse, most of the trail has a very mild grade.

The trail heads west from the parking area toward the red canyon walls before turning north around a ridge. Some shelters and interpretive signs lie along the route. After rounding the ridge, the trail continues west up a broad side canyon. The badlands and bluffs look tempting to climb but be careful. The rock is very soft and crumbly.

At about 1.5 miles or so, the Lighthouse comes into view. Be sure to continue up the trail all the way to it. The last stretch requires a short steep climb up to its base. The Lighthouse is a seventy-five-foot tall pillar of soft shale, capped by an erosion-resistant layer of sandstone. The rock formation is probably the most famous natural landmark of the Texas Panhandle. If you're not acrophobic, be sure to climb up to the top of the headland just behind the Lighthouse. Watch out for crumbly rock near the edge of the cliff.

The trail is good any time of year, but try to get an early start in summer. Winter storm fronts can arrive suddenly, so be aware of weather forecasts.

Although the Lighthouse Trail is the only developed trail in the canyon, don't stop with it. The park contains over 16,000 acres, and many more beautiful rock formations await those willing to hike cross-country. The trail is set up for day hiking only, but the park has several developed campgrounds for overnight stays.

HIKE 28: CAPROCK CANYONS

General description: An easy day hike or overnight trip in the red rock canyons of the the caprock's edge
General location: About ninety miles northeast of Lubbock
Length: About six miles round trip
Elevation: 2,440-3,160 feet
Maps: Caprock Canyons State Park map, Lake Theo 7.5-minute USGS quad
Best season: Fall through spring
Water availability: None
Special attractions: Red rock formations, views
Permit: Required for camping
Finding the trailhead: From Amarillo go south and from Lubbock go north on I-27 to Tulia. Go east on TX 86 about forty-five miles to Quitaque. In Quitaque,

HIKE 28 CAPROCK CANYONS

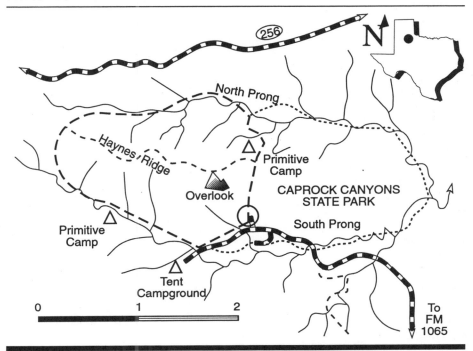

turn left, or north, on FM 1065. The park entrance is on the left about two miles north. The marked trailhead parking area is on the right on the main park road about 4.5 miles into the park. Ignore the two lake turnoffs on the left just past the headquarters building.

The hike: The state park's name comes from the rugged canyons at the edge of the High Plains caprock. To the west lie the high flat plains for which the Texas Panhandle is well-known. To the east the lower plains form a gently rolling land surface. The 1,000-foot drop between the two landforms creates a rugged margin of cliffs and canyons. Most of the exposed rock layers consist of colorful red sandstones and shales of the Quartermaster formation.

The loop trail goes north from the parking lot, climbing through a small gap in a ridge of clay badlands. Sparse vegetation covers the dry country that you pass through. Scrubby one-seed juniper, redberry juniper, and mesquite are lightly scattered across the slopes and flats. In the wetter, narrower canyons, cottonwoods, Rocky Mountain junipers, and occasional oaks grow.

At about a mile, you reach the first of two backcountry campsites. Be sure to obtain a permit ahead of time if you camp. Just before the campsite, an almost unnoticeable trail climbs the steep face of the ridge to the west to the Haynes Ridge Overlook. After the campsite, the trail continues north to the North Prong of the Little Red River. Another trail loop forks off the right. The lower loop is favored by equestrians, but can be added to this loop for a large increase in the described hike's length. Bear left, upstream into the narrowing canyon of the North Prong.

The vegetation becomes lusher, although the creek rarely flows. The trail climbs steeply out of the canyon when it boxes at a normally dry waterfall. Usually enough moisture seeps out in the overhang at the base of the fall to support lush maidenhair ferns. The overhang and luxuriant growth form a cool retreat on a hot summer day.

After climbing out of the North Prong, the trail crosses the top of Haynes Ridge. Tremendous views spread out below of the canyons. A side trail forks left, or east, and follows the ridgetop to the overlook at the end of the ridge. The trail to the overlook adds about four miles round trip or can be used as an alternate return route.

The trail leaves the ridgetop and descends steeply into the South Prong of the Little Red River. After good rains, the creek sometimes runs at least part way down the canyon. About halfway down the canyon, the trail passes the second primitive campsite. Unfortunately, the primitive camps are too close to the beginning and end of the hike, instead of being out at the halfway point.

After about another mile, the trail ends at the parking lot for the tent camping area. Follow the road east for a little less than a mile to complete the loop to the trailhead.

The hike can be hot in summer, but shade in the canyons and low humidity make the trip worthwhile anyway. If you don't backpack in, the park has a developed campground with showers and other amenities. It's easy to spend a couple of days here; Caprock Canyons and Palo Duro Canyon are probably the two most scenic spots in the Panhandle.

HIKE 29: *MONAHANS SANDHILLS*

General description: An easy dayhike through a field of dunes
General location: About six miles northeast of Monahans
Length: About two miles round trip
Elevation: 2,730-2,780 feet
Maps: State park brochure, Cowden Place 7.5-minute USGS quad
Best season: Fall through spring
Water availability: Trailhead
Special attractions: Sand dunes
Finding the trailhead: From Monahans, drive northeast on I-20 about six miles to the exit for Monahans Sandhills State Park. Drive into the park on Park Road 41. Ignore the righthand turn to the first picnic area and turn right into the second picnic area at the concession building and windmill. Park in the large lot at the picnic area.

The hike: The dunes in the state park are only part of a massive dune field that stretches for over 200 miles, from south of Monahans to southeastern New Mexico. In most areas, the dunes are stabilized by vegetation, but the park contains a large area of active, shifting dunes. Although the park appears to be

HIKE 29 *MONAHANS SANDHILLS*

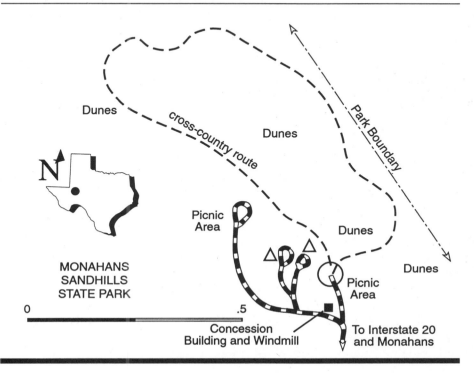

dry desert, just beneath the surface lies a very shallow aquifer of fresh water. With adequate rainfall, the water table is often high enough to form pools in low areas between the dunes. The water attracted man as far back as 12,000 years ago. The white man avoided the area for many years because of the difficulty of travel in sand. However, in the 1880s, the Texas and Pacific Railroad laid tracks through the area and selected Monahans as a stop because of the availability of water. Oil was discovered in the area in the 1920s, leading to development over much of the large Permian Basin.

This hike doesn't follow a formal route and the two mile length is arbitrary. Head out of the north side of the parking lot into the dunes. Go a mile or so and then head back to the parking lot in a big loop. Two miles of hiking in sand is farther than you think. Here and there the dunes are stabilized by a miniature forest of oaks. These oaks are fully mature, even though they rarely exceed four feet in height. Their acorns are surprisingly large for such a small tree.

If you are good at route finding, hike as far out into the dunes as you desire. The windmill at the concession building will help keep you from getting lost if you don't range too far. Be sure to take a compass if you get out of site of the windmill. Dunes can also be reached from the other picnic areas. The dunes are hot in summer and can be windy in spring.

HIKE 30: *ENCHANTED ROCK*

General description: An easy day hike onto and around a large granite dome
General location: About seventeen miles north of Fredericksburg
Length: About five miles round trip
Elevation: 1,360-1,825 feet
Maps: Enchanted Rock State Natural Area Trail Map, Enchanted Rock and Crabapple 7.5-minute USGS quads
Best season: Fall through spring
Water availability: Trailhead
Special attractions: Pink granite dome, rock climbing
Permit: Required for camping
Finding the trailhead: From Fredericksburg, go north on RM 965 about 17.5 miles to the park on the left. Turn in and drive past headquarters and across the creek into the attractive tent-only campground. Turn right at the fork and go to the parking lots at the end of the road.

The hike: The enormous granite dome of Enchanted Rock makes it one of the most interesting sites in Texas. The dome is part of an ancient igneous batholith that covers about 100 square miles of the central mineral region of Texas. The granite is one of the oldest exposed rocks in North America, with an estimated age of one billion years. The high-grade stone is quarried at various sites for use as a building material. Unfortunately, one noisy quarry lies just across the park boundary on the north side. I hope that in future the park can acquire more land as a buffer.

The main dome, Enchanted Rock proper, is one of many outcrops both within

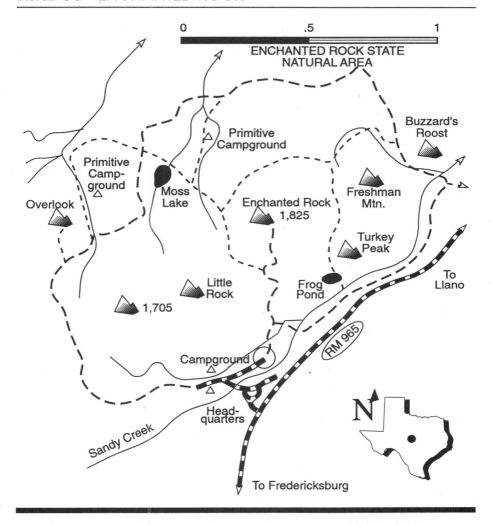

and outside of the park. With an abrupt rise of several hundred feet and a largely bare rock surface, the dome gives tremendous views of the surrounding hill country. The rock is important not only geologically but also supports several rare plants.

This hike will follow the main loop trail, plus a side trip up to the summit of the dome. The broad trail starts from the loop at the end of the road and drops down into Sandy Creek. Signs mark a junction in the creek bottom. The loop trail goes right, down the wash, while the summit trail climbs straight north up the dome. Anyone who visits Enchanted Rock will be unable to resist climbing the dome, so follow the summit trail for now. Once you get up onto the bare rock surface, just charge straight ahead until you're on the highest point. Enjoy the view.

After you tire of watching the vultures circling high above, retreat back down to the loop trail and continue the counter-clockwise circle of the rock. The park is very popular, so many unofficial trails have been worn. Don't worry if you lose the main route. With the dome and other rocks, such as Turkey Peak, Freshman Mountain, and Buzzard's Roost, constantly in view, you won't get lost. Occasional signs also help.

The loop trail follows Sandy Creek downstream for almost a mile before turning northwest between Buzzard's Roost and Freshman Mountain. The trail then turns west and travels below the north side on the main dome. If the weather is good, expect to see rock climbers all over the sheer north face. The granite makes one of the best climbing rocks in Texas.

The trail continues southwest, finally looping around Little Rock and back into the campground. If you want a campsite for a spring or fall weekend, be sure to reserve several weeks ahead; the park is very popular. The three backcountry camp areas are usually not as difficult to reserve. Summers are usually hot, but if you start early, you'll still enjoy the hike.

Don't feel limited to the described route of this hike. Several other trails cut across the loop. The bare rock domes are irresistible in themselves. Climb up and down at will.

HIKE 31: *COLORADO BEND*

General description: An easy day hike through typical oak-juniper Hill Country
General location: About forty miles northeast of Llano
Length: About four miles round trip
Elevation: 1,320-1,425 feet
Maps: Colorado Bend State Park map, Bend and Gorman Falls 7.5-minute USGS quads
Best season: Fall through spring
Water availability: See text
Special attractions: Lush Hill Country grassland
Permit: Required for camping
Finding the trailhead: From Llano, drive north on Texas 16 about seventeen miles to Cherokee. Turn right on RM 501 and go about sixteen miles to the junction with FM 580. Go right on FM 580 about 1.3 miles to the village of Bend. Continue straight onto a gravel road in the middle of town, rather than making the sharp turn left on FM 580 over the Colorado River bridge. Small signs for Colorado Bend State Park mark the start of the gravel road. Follow the gravel road into the park, following state park signs at junctions. The marked trailhead is on the right at about 5.1 miles. The gravel road is easily passable by any vehicle, although it gets rougher once you enter the park.

The hike: Colorado Bend State Park is a relatively new state park that is still almost undiscovered. Little development has been done to date; roads are still

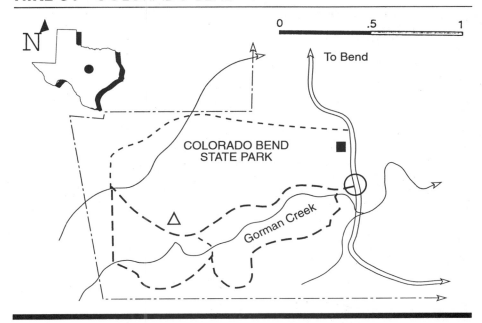

unpaved and the formal campground has only tables and chemical toilets. However, if you like quiet and lack of crowds, this park is for you. The park lies on a bend of the Colorado River at the very upper end of Lake Buchanan. Boats from the lake can usually navigate at least part way upstream through the park. A narrow wooded floodplain lines the river, then steep bluffs rise up into gently rolling uplands.

This hike winds through open upland terrain dotted here and there with clumps of oak and juniper. The lack of recent grazing has led to thick, lush grassland, similar to what once covered much of the Texas Hill Country. For the most part the trail follows old, mostly overgrown ranch roads. The old road starts west from the parking area and reaches a fork, marked by a rock cairn and small blue trail markers, in only 100 yards or so. Go left and wind through open Hill Country for about 1.3 miles to another junction.

The fork, another old road, cuts sharply back to the left. Rock cairns mark the turnoff. Take the fork. You'll know that you are on the right route when you pass a steel tank on the left in about .25 mile and a dirt stock pond in about .5 mile. At a total distance of about 2.4 miles you may or may not see a faint unmarked road cutting back to the left. Ignore it and continue on about fifty yards to the proper junction. Turn right at the obvious T-shaped junction. By going left, you can lengthen the loop by about .4 mile. See the map.

The trail passes the marked primitive camping area and a windmill on the left. The windmill tank was full of water when I hiked this trail, but I wouldn't count on it without inquiring before your hike. On this short a walk I would carry water rather than purifying it.

Just past the windmill lies another set of primitive camping area signs. Look at the large mesquite tree by the signs for the blue and yellow plastic trail markers. Turn left off the old road and follow the small blue triangles that point the way. This leg of the hike can be hard to follow, since it's little used. Look closely and follow the blue markers nailed to stumps and trees. Frequent rock cairns also help with route finding. The trail is most easily lost when it turns, so look all around for the markers. If you lose the trail, retrace your route and use the map to follow the more obvious fork back to the trailhead.

The route becomes clearer after a while as it joins a faint old road. The road leads straight back to the trailhead, passing the first fork of the loop on the right just before the parking area.

Mountain bikers can also use this trail, although from what I saw very few people at all are using it. Go now before everyone else and enjoy an easy walk through empty Hill Country. Soon after this book goes to print, the park should have opened walks to the spectacular travertine cascades of Gorman Falls and the dark, winding tunnel of Gorman Cave. Be sure not to miss them.

HIKE 32: *SPICEWOOD SPRINGS*

General description: A moderate day hike through the Texas Hill Country
General location: About forty-five miles northeast of Llano
Length: About five miles round trip
Elevation: 1,020-1,320 feet
Maps: Colorado Bend State Park map, Gorman Falls 7.5-minute USGS quad
Best season: Fall through spring
Water availability: Park campground, Spicewood Creek
Special attractions: Colorado River, travertine pools and cascades, swimming hole
Finding the trailhead: From Llano, drive north on TX 16 about seventeen miles to Cherokee. Turn right on RM 501 and go about sixteen miles to the junction with FM 580. Go right on FM 580 about 1.3 miles to the village of Bend. Continue straight onto a gravel road in the middle of town, rather than making the sharp turn left on FM 580 over the Colorado River bridge. Small signs for Colorado Bend State Park mark the start of the gravel road. Follow the gravel road into the park, following state park signs at junctions. At about 10.1 miles along the gravel road, the road forks at park headquarters on the river. Turn right and drive another .4 mile to the end of the road at the boat ramp. The gravel road is easily passable by any vehicle, although it gets rougher once you enter the park.

The hike: So far, Colorado Bend State Park has escaped discovery by the hordes of Austin, Dallas, and San Antonio hikers. If you visit on a weekday, you may have the park to yourself. Not only is the park newly opened, it has few of the developed facilities of most of the state parks. There are no paved roads, fishing piers, or showers. Enjoy it. The status quo probably won't last forever.

The park lies on the banks of the Colorado River at the very upstream end of Lake Buchanan. Steep wooded hillsides of oak and juniper tumble down to the

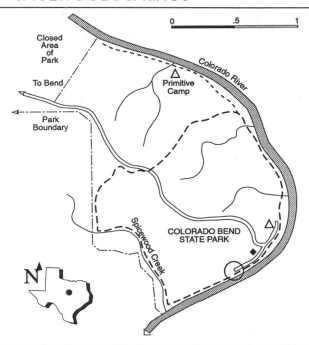

lush narrow river floodplain. This trail passes through most of the park habitats, from the river floodplain to the Hill Country uplands. I recommend some parts of this trail only to experienced hikers, so read the entire description before starting out.

This trail follows a loop, so start by walking the .4 mile back up the road to park headquarters. From headquarters, continue along the road by the river into and through the campground. Cross the gate at the far end of the campground and continue along an old road that follows the river floodplain. The floodplain is beautiful, with large oaks, pecans, and elms lining the road.

About a mile past the campground, the old road enters a broad, open section of the floodplain. At the sign indicating that the primitive camping area is further up the road, turn left. Look for the sign at the edge of the floodplain marking the trail. If you are an inexperienced hiker, don't attempt this part of the trail. It's too easy to get lost. Instead continue another mile or so up the floodplain road until you hit the closed part of the park and then return the same way.

The trail climbing up the hill behind the sign is new and has not been improved at this writing. After more work has been done, the trail should be easier to follow and my warnings will no longer apply. At present, the trail is only a route marked by survey flagging on trees and occasional rock cairns. Watch carefully to avoid losing the route. A compass and topo map will help. The trail simply climbs up to the park entrance road that follows Lemons Ridge

Armadillos are common in much of Texas.

about a mile away. If you get lost, just go downhill. Sooner or later you will always end up back at the river.

The trail climbs through scrubby oak-juniper woodland and reaches the road and ridgetop at a marked trailhead parking area.

Turn right and walk up the road about 100 yards to another trail sign on the left. The next section of trail is a little easier to follow. The trail, a faint old road, goes off to the right from behind the sign. It forks fairly quickly; bear left and follow the occasional survey flag. Follow the old road gently downhill into the Spicewood Creek drainage. After a while the old road roughly follows the park boundary fence. The road hits the small running creek about a mile from the ridgetop. The old road gets faint toward the end. If you lose it, just continue downhill and you will soon hit the creek.

The hike down the creek is very scenic with water tumbling down small cascades into pools dammed with travertine. Purify any water that you take from the creek and be careful not to break the travertine dams or trample the delicate streamside vegetation. Dense forest shades much of the route. Since there is no improved trail, this is the roughest part of the hike. You won't get lost hiking down the creek, but you will have to bushwhack. After about a mile the creek joins the Colorado River. Just above the river, the creek forms a beautiful deep, clear swimming hole, perfect after a sweaty hike. From the confluence, follow an old road up the river floodplain about .7 mile to the trailhead.

The trail described here is new and thus rough and difficult to follow. With time the park will probably improve it, so be sure to ask ahead of time. Until then, inexperienced hikers should stick with the trail along the river.

HIKE 33: PEDERNALES FALLS

General description: An easy day hike through the undeveloped Hill Country of Pedernales Falls State Park

General location: About forty miles west of Austin

Length: About 6.5 miles round trip

Elevation: 780-1,040 feet

Maps: Pedernales Falls State Park hikers map, Hammetts Crossing 7.5-minute USGS quad

Best season: All year

Water availability: Trailhead, Pedernales River

Special attractions: Hill Country river

Finding the trailhead: Drive west on US 290 about 24 miles from the TX 71/US 290 junction on the southwest side of Austin. Turn right, or north, on RM 3232 and drive about 6.6 miles to the Pedernales Falls State Park entrance at the junction with RM 2766. Drive into the park about 3.4 miles to the paved turnoff on the right marked with the campground sign. Drive into the campground and go right at the two forks. At about .8 mile park in the lot marked with the "River Trail" sign. Don't stop at the nature trail parking lot just before it.

The hike: Pedernales Falls State Park is one of the closest hiking areas to Austin and San Antonio. The park lies in typical rolling Hill Country—limestone hills wooded with a scrub forest of oak and juniper. The crystal-clear Pedernales River winds its way through the park in a canyon lined with rocky bluffs. Bald cypresses, veterans of many floods, line the banks of the river. Normally, I wouldn't recommend a Hill Country hike in summer, but this one is an exception. If you start early, you can be back at the river by the time it gets really hot. Jump right in and cool off!

Initially the trail heads downhill to the river. Most of the hike is on old ranch roads used occasionally by park vehicles. A short way down, the trail forks at some signs warning of flood hazards. Go right and stay with the old road. Cross the river on the road crossing and climb up the far bank past the flood warning siren mounted on a pole. As you have probably gathered by now, the Pedernales River has had catastrophic floods in the past. Pay attention to the weather and any warnings or sirens.

The route can be somewhat confusing once you climb up out of the river. Follow the directions and map carefully and consider taking a topographic map. If you do get lost, just backtrack until you are oriented. If you are unable to backtrack, just go downhill and you will soon hit the river. Walk upstream along the river and you will find either the road crossing or the developed area around the falls.

Several faint roads fork off of the proper route, but unless the directions say otherwise, follow the most traveled route and you will have no trouble. The loop is easier to follow counterclockwise, as I describe it here. A little over a mile after you have climbed up out of the river, the road makes a fairly sharp bend left around a hill. There is faint road going to the right from the point of the sharp

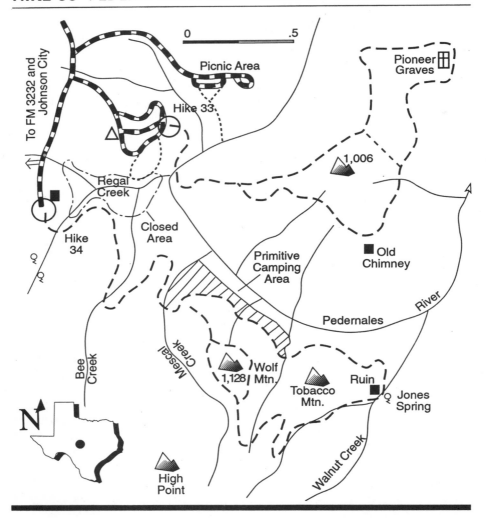

turn. If you want to see the old ruined chimney and corral left by some early pioneers, follow the faint track about seventy-five yards or so. The corral is usually easier to find than the chimney. Return to the main road after the side trip.

A bit less than .5 mile past the corral and chimney, you'll see an old stone wall on the right. Just past the wall is a junction. Stay left on the more worn route. In only a few more yards, a faint road forks left. This route cuts off the outer part of the loop (see the map) if you want to shorten the hike. The main road continues for close to another mile or so before hitting the boundary fence. Turn left and follow the fence line up the hill. An old pioneer cemetery lies in a shady grove of oaks and junipers on the left. The old overgrown graveyard is a peaceful, melancholy place.

The trail (not a road anymore) continues up the hill along the fence past the cemetery and reaches the highest point of the hike. At the top the trail turns left and follows the fence down across a broad, grassy drainage. At the top of the other side of the drainage, the trail hits another old ranch road. Go left, or south, on the old road. After about .5 mile, you will pass the shortcut route on the left. Finally you'll hit the end of the loop at a "Y." Continue straight ahead, downhill to the river.

Although summers are usually hot and humid, a swim in the river will quickly cool you down. The rest of the year is cooler and more pleasant. Insects may sometimes be a nuisance, mainly in late spring and early summer along the river and creeks. Be sure to visit the falls while you're in the park. If you have time, take the short nature trail from the other trailhead in the campground. The trail overlooks the hidden oasis of Bee Creek.

HIKE 34: *WOLF MOUNTAIN*

General description: A moderately easy day hike through the Hill Country above the Pedernales River
General location: About forty miles west of Austin
Length: About seven miles round trip
Elevation: 900-1,090 feet
Maps: Pedernales Falls State Park hikers map, Hammetts Crossing and Pedernales Falls 7.5-minute USGS quads
Best season: Fall through spring
Water availability: Jones Spring, Pedernales River
Special attractions: Hill Country river, views
Permit: Required for camping
Finding the trailhead: Drive west on US 290 about twenty-four miles from the TX 71/US 290 junction on the southwest side of Austin. Turn right, or north, on RM 3232 and drive about 6.6 miles to the Pedernales Falls State Park entrance at the junction with RM 2766. Drive into the park about three miles to the paved turnoff on the right marked with a primitive camping area sign. Drive down the side road about .2 mile to its end and park.

The hike: The 4,800-acre Pedernales Falls State Park is one of the closest backpacking escapes from Austin. The crystal-clear Pedernales River winds its way through the park in a canyon lined with rocky bluffs. Falls and cascades on the river are a popular attraction on the north side of the park. Side canyons with intermittent streams shelter tall oaks, elms, and cypresses. The uplands are generally wooded with a scrub forest of juniper and oak, typical for the Hill Country.

Initially the trail heads straight south into a dense patch of juniper but soon pops out onto a three-way dirt road closed to vehicles. Continue south, the same direction, and follow the signs. Most of the hike is on a dirt road used occasionally by park vehicles.

At about one mile, the trail crosses Bee Creek. The creek cuts a narrow rocky canyon that is lined with bald cypresses downstream from the trail. At about 1.75 miles, the trail crosses Mescal Creek. A sign at the creek shows the boundaries of the primitive camping area (Mescal Creek, Tobacco Creek, the rock bluffs above the river, and the trail). Just beyond the sign, ignore the trail going left along Mescal Creek into the camping area and stay with the main trail. Turn right, uphill, about 200 or 300 yards past Mescal Creek and start the loop trail. The trail climbs at a moderate grade up Wolf Mountain to another junction in about .25 mile.

Take either fork at the junction; they rejoin in less than .5 mile on the other side of Wolf Mountain. I prefer the left fork because it provides excellent views of the Pedernales River valley. A little past where the two routes rejoin, the trail finally turns into a real trail, rather than a dirt road.

At a little over three miles, the trail drops into a fork of Walnut Creek. The trail winds through dense woods along the dry creek for the next half mile and is probably the most scenic part of the hike. Look closely at the huge, gnarled live oak at the first creek crossing. A prickly pear is growing in its main crotch. After leaving the creek, the trail passes several crumbling stone walls built by early settlers.

The ruins of an old ranch house lie right above Jones Spring. The spring trickles down a narrow, fern-lined, rocky canyon. Walk on the rocks to avoid trampling the delicate vegetation. Water can be obtained here, as well as from the river, but be sure to treat it.

After leaving the old ranch, the trail turns back west toward the trailhead. The trail crosses Tobacco Creek at about 4.5 miles and follows the edge of the primitive camping area. All the little trails going down to the right lead into the camping area. Be sure to walk down through the camping area to the bluffs and scramble down to the river. A swim in the cool clear running river is irresistible on a hot summer day. Be aware of the weather, especially in the spring. Because of its overgrazed watershed, the Pedernales floods easily.

The trail passes some pit toilets in the center of the camping area before meeting the other fork of the loop near Mescal Creek. Follow the same route back to the trailhead.

Although summers are usually hot and humid, a swim in the river quickly washes off the sweat. The rest of the year is cooler and even more pleasant. Insects may sometimes be bothersome, mainly in late spring and early summer along the river and creeks. Be sure to visit the falls while you're in the park.

HIKE 35: *LOST MAPLES*

General description: An easy day hike through bigtooth maples in a narrow Hill Country canyon
General location: About fifty miles southwest of Kerrville
Length: About 4.6 miles round trip
Elevation: 1,800-2,250 feet

Maps: Lost Maples State Natural Area map, Sabinal Canyon 7.5-minute USGS quad
Best season: All year
Water availability: Trailhead, seasonal creeks
Special attractions: Fall maples, deep canyons
Permit: Required for camping
Finding the trailhead: Several approaches are possible. From Kerrville, drive about thirty-five miles west on TX 39 to RM 187. Go left on RM 187 about fifteen miles to the Lost Maples State Natural Area entrance on the right. Drive through the park to the large parking lot at the end of the paved road.

The hike: Lost Maples State Natural Area lies in one of the most beautiful parts of the Texas Hill Country. Deeper canyons than usual cut the area into very hilly country. Even better, Lost Maples is far enough from Austin and San Antonio to escape the endless development that covers so much of the Hill Country. The park is famous for the bigtooth maples that line the deeper canyons in and around the park. Only a few other areas in Texas have the maples, mostly in the West Texas mountains.

Because bigtooth maples usually have the best fall color in Texas, the park can be jammed with people on weekends in late October and early November. During fall color, try to come on weekdays. The rest of the year the park is only lightly visited.

The well-marked trail starts from the end of the parking lot and follows up the Sabinal River canyon. Usually only a small stream flows, making it very easy to cross with dry feet. Water levels vary with rainfall and are generally highest in late spring. Water, if purified, can usually be obtained from the streams, but carrying water is probably a better choice.

The trail forks soon after starting. The two forks rejoin within .5 mile; they just follow opposite creek banks. I recommend the left fork, or Maple Trail, because of its heavy concentration of mature maples. The trails rejoin when the Maple Trail crosses the creek and meets the other trail. At a little less than 1.5 miles, at a fork in the canyon, the trail crosses the creek at an interesting area of cliffs and rock ledges. Just after the crossing lies the first primitive camp area (Area "A") with its composting toilet. A beautiful stand of maples lines the creek at the camp area.

The most beautiful part of the hike lies just beyond the camp area in Hale Hollow Creek. The canyon becomes very narrow and steep-walled with many maples. After following the creek for a short distance, the trail climbs steeply out of the canyon and onto a ridge. You reach the top at about two miles. A junction is reached about .25 mile further. Unless you're tired or short on time, take the dead-end left fork less than .5 mile to an overlook that provides a good view down the Sabinal River Canyon. Return to the junction and continue along the right fork.

The trail follows the ridge top to another junction at almost three miles. The right fork goes a short distance to primitive camp area "B." Go left, and drop down a short steep stretch to a large pond along Can Creek. Another camp area ("C") and composting toilet are by the pond. A well-marked trail junction also

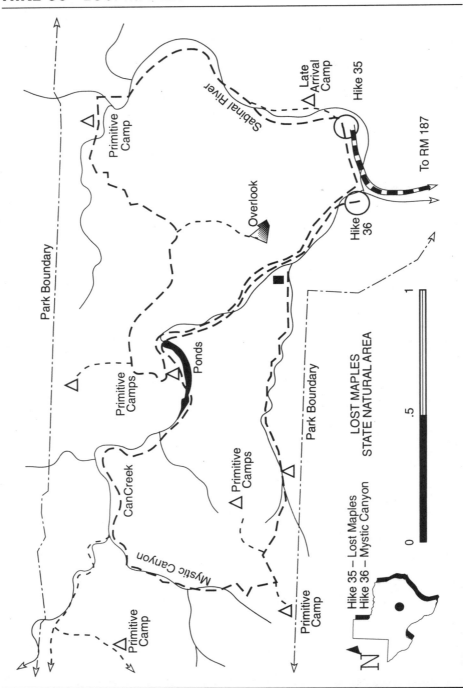

Late
Arrival
Camp

Hike 35

Sabinal River

Primitive
Camp

To RM 187

Overlook

Hike
36

Park Boundary

Ponds

Primitive
Camps

Park Boundary

CanCreek

Primitive
Camps

Mystic Canyon

Primitive
Camp

Primitive
Camp

LOST MAPLES
STATE NATURAL AREA

0   .5   1

Hike 35 – Lost Maples
Hike 36 – Mystic Canyon

N

lies in the canyon bottom by the pond. The right fork makes another loop through the park (See Hike #36). Go left, downstream. Walk down the canyon, passing another trail fork on the right and some park buildings. A little over a mile downstream from the pond, you will hit a gravel parking area at the confluence of Can Creek and the Sabinal River. Walk down the road, cross the river, and turn left on the paved road. In less than .5 mile, you will hit the trailhead parking lot.

The hike is pleasant anytime of year. In spring and summer, insects can be a nuisance. Summers are usually hot and humid. Spring and fall probably provide the best camping weather. Although the hike can easily be done in a day, try to stay overnight to enjoy the narrow canyon country.

HIKE 36: *MYSTIC CANYON*

General description: An easy day hike through the rugged Hill Country of Lost Maples State Natural Area
General location: About fifty miles southwest of Kerrville
Length: About 4.5 miles round trip
Elevation: 1,800-2,260 feet
Maps: Lost Maples State Natural Area map, Sabinal Canyon 7.5-minute USGS quad
Best season: All year
Water availability: Seasonal in Can Creek
Special attractions: Bigtooth maples, rugged Hill Country canyons
Permit: Required for camping
Finding the trailhead: Follow the directions to the park for Hike 35, but turn left across the Sabinal River to the Can Creek trailhead and overflow parking area about .75 mile into the park from the entrance.

The hike: Lost Maples State Natural Area is most famous for its stands of bigtooth maples. The trees turn brilliant shades of gold and scarlet in fall in good years. The maples grow in only a few areas of the Texas Hill Country, with most in the deep canyons in and around the park. The canyons are deeper and narrower than most areas of the Hill Country and apparently provide conditions favorable to the maples' growth.

The park, in one of the least-developed areas of the Hill Country, contains about ten miles of hiking trails. The trails provide one of the best opportunities to see wild country in central Texas.

From the large gravel parking area, follow the dirt road up Can Creek. The well-marked trail is a road for the first half mile or so. The road is closed to all but park vehicles. At a bit less than .5 mile, at a fork in the canyon with several park buildings, the trail forks. The right fork will be the end of the loop hike. Go left, up the side canyon and climb at a mild grade. The canyon is quite steep-walled and narrow, with good stands of maples. At about 1.5 miles, the trail passes primitive camping area "D." A half mile beyond, the trail makes a short, fairly steep climb out of the canyon onto a ridge. The ridge tops are less protected and the vegetation is sparser and drier than in the canyons. The maples generally concentrate in canyon bottoms and north-facing slopes.

The trail forks soon after reaching the top. The right fork goes a short distance to primitive camping area "F." A composting toilet lies near the junction. Continue along the ridge top on the left fork. Within about 200 yards, another fork goes to the left, to primitive camp area "E." Bear right and make the short, fairly steep descent into Mystic Canyon after about 200 yards. Maples become more common again upon reaching the canyon bottom.

Follow Mystic Canyon downstream to a trail junction at a little less than 2.5 miles. The left fork makes a short loop up another canyon fork. Be sure to take the side trip, less than two miles long, if you have time. It leads to more canyon country and probably the two least-used primitive camp areas. The right fork continues downstream to Can Creek and some ponds. At a little less than 3.5 miles, the trail reaches primitive camp area "C" and a trail fork. The left fork leads to the loop described in Hike 35. Continue downstream, to the right, for about a mile to the trailhead. The start of the loop is passed on the right after a little more than .5 mile.

Parts of this hike and Hike 35 can be combined into one large loop if desired. Water can usually be obtained in the ponds of Can Creek, but carrying water is usually better. Summers are usually hot and humid, but the hike is shady enough to be pleasant. Mosquitoes, ticks, and chiggers should be prepared for, especially in spring and summer. The fall color can be spectacular, but try to avoid weekends; Lost Maples can be packed with people. The park, especially the backcountry, is usually relatively quiet the rest of the year.

HIKE 37: *CIBOLO CREEK*

General description: An easy day hike along a cypress-lined Hill Country stream
General location: Boerne
Length: About two miles round trip
Elevation: 1,350-1,380 feet
Maps: Cibolo Wilderness Trail brochure (City of Boerne), Boerne 7.5-minute USGS quad
Best season: Fall through spring
Water availability: Trailhead
Special attractions: Bald cypresses, native prairie, creek
Finding the trailhead: From the intersection of TX 46 and US 87 in the center of Boerne, go east on TX 46 about 1 mile to a paved turnoff on the right. Signs indicate the city park and Cibolo Wilderness Trail. Drive .4 mile to a fork and go right again. Go .2 mile and park at the pavilion on the right.

The hike: The Cibolo Creek Wilderness is an idyllic retreat hidden away in a forgotten corner of the Boerne City Park. A short, easy trail winds through a small area of native prairie, a marsh, and a cypress-lined creek. The hike makes a quick escape from the urban chaos of nearby San Antonio.

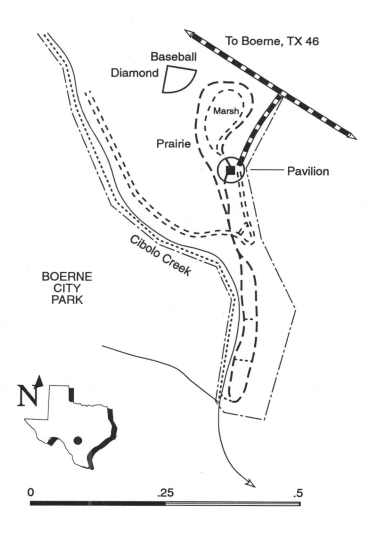

To Boerne, TX 46

Baseball
Diamond

Marsh

Prairie

Pavilion

Cibolo Creek

BOERNE
CITY
PARK

N

0   .25   .5

The trail drops down into the meadow behind the pavilion. Much of the trail is a mowed path through the grass and thus its route may vary somewhat. At the fork below the pavilion, go right, around the trail looping the reclaimed marsh. Boardwalks cross the wettest areas. The trail then circles south through the prairie and away from the baseball diamonds to the north. The trail meets the other side of the loop at the far side of the meadow and continues south to a dirt park road. Go right on it a very short distance to the creek. Go downstream along the creek, at first on the road, then back onto the trail.

The trail follows the stream, lined with large bald cypresses, to the park boundary at a fence crossing the creek. Along the way you will pass two old stone stairways climbing the bank to the left. They just shortcut up to the other side of the loop. At the fence, the trail climbs up the left bank and loops back upstream along the top of the stream bank. At the end of the creek loop, follow the same route back to the pavilion, or follow the dirt park road back.

The hike back can be altered by using stepping stones to cross the creek at the boundary fence and following another trail back upstream along the creek on the far bank. Near the north end of the park, recross the creek and cross the meadow area to the pavilion.

The park is small and the trail short, but Cibolo Creek is a very scenic, tranquil spot in the Hill Country.

Bald cypresses line Cibolo Creek in the Texas Hill Country.

HIKE 38   *INKS LAKE*

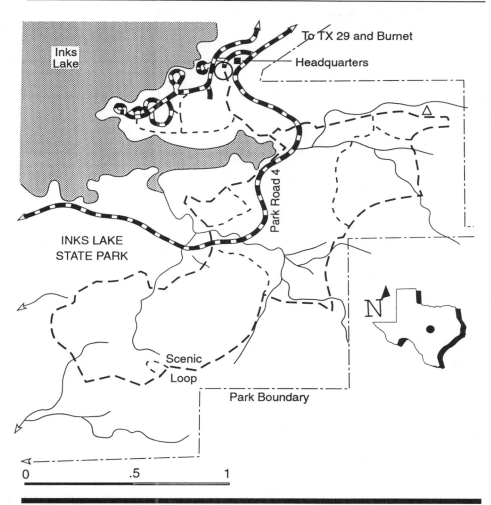

HIKE 38: *INKS LAKE*

General description: An easy day hike through the granite hills of Inks Lake State Park

General location: About twenty miles northwest of Marble Falls

Length: About five miles round trip

Elevation: 890-1,020 feet

Maps: Inks Lake State Park Hiking Trail map, Longhorn Cavern and Kingsland 7.5-minute USGS quads

Best season: Fall through spring

Water availability: Trailhead

Special attractions: Granite hills, spring wildflowers

Permits: Required for camping

Finding the trailhead: Drive north about 8.3 miles on US 281 from Marble Falls. Turn left on Park Road 4 and drive about 12.8 miles to the entrance of Inks Lake State Park. Drive into the park past the headquarters building. The Pecan Flat trailhead is at the marked gravel parking lot adjoining the large paved headquarters parking lot.

The hike: Inks Lake lies in the heart of the area known as the Llano Uplift. Most of the Texas Hill Country consists of sedimentary limestone layers, but much of the area surrounding Llano and Marble Falls lies on top of an enormous mass of ancient granite. The high grade pinkish granite is quarried in several areas for construction uses. The Texas capitol building is one of the more famous users of the stone. The Inks Lake trail winds through low hills of the attractive rock.

From the gravel parking lot, start down the trail behind the large trail sign. Ignore the unofficial trail forking off to the right after only about fifty yards. After about .2 mile go left at the first official fork toward the main loop. The next fork, after another .2 mile, starts the main loop.

This hike follows the main outer loop for a total hike of just over five miles. As is obvious from the map, many shorter sub-loops are possible. To stay on the main outer loop, just turn left at every junction until you return to the start of the loop. To prevent confusion at the multiple junctions, the park has installed small trail maps with "You are here" markers at almost every intersection. The trail crosses Park Road 4 twice.

The trail is surprisingly little used considering the heavy use received by the developed parts of the park. As shown on the map, the trail encounters the primitive camp area a short distance into the main loop. The attractive campsites and a chemical toilet lie on the densely wooded floodplain of a small creek.

When the trail crosses bare granite it can be hard to follow. However, generally the park has marked the route in such places with wooden markers, rock cairns, and lines of rocks. Look carefully and you shouldn't have any trouble. The southwest side of the loop, especially the small scenic loop (see map) probably has the best views. In spring, the wildflowers can be especially attractive sprinkled across the pink granite.

HIKE 39: *BARTON CREEK*

General description: A moderate day hike through a surprisingly wild area within Austin

General location: Austin

Length: About sixteen miles round trip

Elevation: 460-880 feet

Maps: Hike and Bike Trails of Austin (Austin Parks and Recreation Department), Austin West and Oak Hill 7.5-minute USGS quads

Best season: Fall through spring

Water availability: Trailhead (Zilker Park)

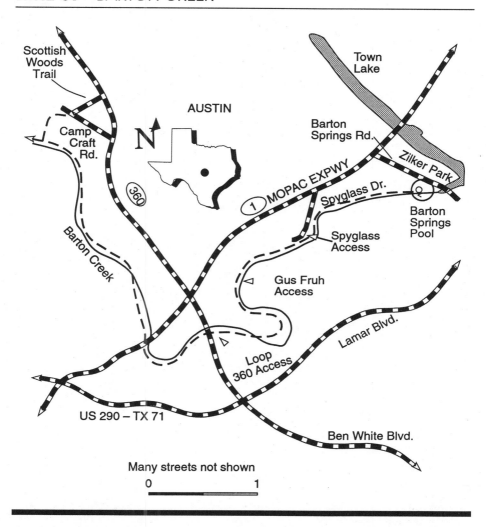

Scottish Woods Trail

Town Lake

Camp Craft Rd.

AUSTIN

N

Barton Springs Rd.

Zilker Park

360

MOPAC EXPWY

1

Spyglass Dr.

Barton Springs Pool

Barton Creek

Spyglass Access

Gus Fruh Access

Lamar Blvd.

Loop 360 Access

US 290 – TX 71

Ben White Blvd.

Many streets not shown

0   1

Special attractions: Rugged, wooded Hill Country canyon, accessibility
Finding the trailhead: The trail winds through West Austin and has multiple trailheads, making hikes of various lengths possible. One of the easiest to find (and the one described as the starting point for this hike) lies in Zilker Park. Zilker Park lies on the south side of Town Lake in the center of the city on Barton Springs Road, between South First Street and TX Loop 1 (informally known as MoPac). Follow the signs in Zilker Park to Barton Springs Pool. Finding a spot to park can be difficult on summer weekends.

The hike: In spring and early summer Barton Creek will be a clear running stream, bubbling over cascades into deep pools. Some years, if rains are heavy enough, the creek can be run by tubers and canoeists. The lower part of the creek is usually dry the rest of the year. The winding canyon follows a course from its confluence with Town Lake at Zilker Park far southwest into the Hill Country. The city of Austin acquired much of the land adjoining the creek and protected it from development. The trail system runs about eight miles upstream from Zilker Park.

The trail along the Barton Creek Greenbelt is one of many that follow creeks in Austin. The Barton Creek trail is the longest and least developed trail. From the large swimming pool in Barton Creek, fed by springs, walk upstream to the trailhead just southwest of the pool area. Initially the trail passes through woods along the north side of the creek. On the cliffs above perch expensive houses. The trail is very heavily used, especially on warm weekends. Many side trails and parallel trails have been worn, but regardless, the trail follows the creek all the

Barton Creek plunges over a small cascade.

way upstream. The trail crosses the creek several times along its eight-mile path. After heavy rains it can be difficult to cross, and occasionally even dangerous.

At about 1.25 miles, the side trail to the Spyglass access is on the right. As you progress, the terrain gets wilder, sometimes making the city seem nonexistent. The trail passes through lush woods, dominated by oaks, cedar elms, sycamores, and juniper. At a little over two miles, the Gus Fruh access trail goes to the left. At about 3.75 miles, the trail passes the TX Loop 360 access trail on the left. There is a restroom at the Loop 360 trailhead. This access point is easily found on the north side of Loop 360 between TX Loop 1 and Lamar Boulevard.

The trail beyond Loop 360 becomes even wilder and gets less and less used (although it is still quite popular). It passes under the high Loop 1 bridge a short distance past the Loop 360 bridge. At about six miles, after the trail has turned into a small dirt road, at least a small amount of water usually appears in the creek, even in the dry season. Two small cascades form great swimming holes. At about 7.5 miles, the canyon widens into a broad park-like area with a restroom. The trail continues a short distance upstream on the right side before ending. A trail climbs up to the north out of the canyon (the only steep part of the hike) to the upper access point in the Woods of Westlake subdivision. The marked trail hits the subdivision near the intersection of Camp Craft Road and Scottish Woods Trail.

This is a beautiful hike, even if it lies in a large city. Ideally hikers should set up a car shuttle and cut the round trip length in half. Many mountain bikers use the trail, so be alert for the occasional reckless rider. With its city location and heavy use, the trail is not designed for camping. Use care crossing the creek if it's running high. Floods are not uncommon in spring. In summer, if you set up a car shuttle, start your hike at the top and jump into the enormous Barton Springs Pool at the end.

HIKE 40: *LOST PINES*

General description: A moderately easy day hike or overnight trip in the Lost Pines of Texas
General location: Bastrop State Park, just east of Bastrop
Length: About 8.5 miles round trip
Elevation: 390-570 feet
Maps: Bastrop State Park hiking map, Bastrop and Smithville 7.5-minute USGS quads
Best season: Fall through spring
Water availability: None
Special attractions: Dense pine forest
Permit: Required for camping
Finding the trailhead: Go east of Bastrop on TX 21 for about a mile. The Bastrop State Park entrance is at the intersection of TX 21 and TX Loop 150. Drive into the park past the entrance station and golf course. At about .7 mile, go right on Park Road 1A. Drive about 1.2 miles on Park Road 1A to the well-marked

trailhead on the right. The parking area is on the left about .1 miles further down the road.

The hike: Bastrop State Park is in the heart of the Lost Pines, an island of loblolly pines separated from the main body of the East Texas pine forests by about 100 miles. The isolated patch of pine-oak woodland is the most westerly in Texas. Texas becomes drier from east to west, with most pines growing in lush East Texas. The Lost Pines survive in their drier location because of a geologic formation of sandstone and sand conducive to their growth. The pines end abruptly at the boundaries of the sandy soil.

Bastrop State Park was established in the Lost Pines in 1938 with an area of 2,100 acres. Many of the rustic old buildings and facilities were built by the CCC of stone and hand-hewn lumber. In 1979, an additional 1,450 acres were added to the park. The trail makes a large beautiful loop through lush pine-oak forest.

The well-maintained trail starts by crossing a small intermittent creek in dense pine forest. The first hundred yards or so pass through what appears to have been a picnic area in the past. Frequent aluminum rectangles nailed to trees mark the trail throughout its route. The tilt of the rectangles indicates the trail direction.

At about .6 mile, you will hit a well-marked trail junction. Go right, toward the Buescher Junction. This is the start of the loop; you will return here via the

HIKE 40 *LOST PINES*

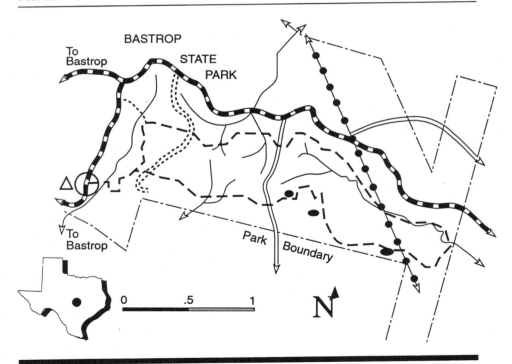

other fork. In less than .25 mile, you will cross a primitive dirt road. Backcountry camping is allowed to the east of the road.

You cross a fence about 200 yards past the primitive road. At 1.7 miles, you cross a gravel county road. To cut the loop short, you can go left on the road to the other side of the loop. At a pond at about three miles, the trail may get a bit confusing. Follow around the left, or north side, of the pond to find the trail. The trail crosses a power line right-of-way just past the pond.

At 3.9 miles you hit another marked junction. The right fork, still under construction, will eventually connect with Buescher State Park to the east (See Hike 41). Bear left and continue around the loop. The area around and past the junction is the most scenic part of the hike, with deep gullies and the largest pines.

At a little over 4.5 miles, you recross the power line right of way. At about 6.1 miles, you recross the gravel road. At about 6.75 miles, you recross the fence and the primitive road, and leave the back country camping area. At about 7.3 miles the trail reaches the well-marked Overlook Junction. Go left, back toward the Trailhead Junction. The right fork leads .4 mile to a second trailhead.

At about 7.9 miles, you hit the first junction and the end of the loop. Retrace the last .6 mile to the trailhead. Watch out for poison ivy on this trail. The trail passes through heavily wooded terrain with no landmarks. Be careful if you leave the trail; it's easy to get lost. The park is fairly small, so you would hit a road before too long, but getting lost would at least be a nuisance. Ticks, mosquitoes, and chiggers are common, especially from spring through summer. Summers tend to be hot and humid. The park has developed campgrounds and even rustic cabins that can be rented. The hike is an excellent opportunity to see the beautiful Lost Pines of Texas.

HIKE 41: BUESCHER STATE PARK

General description: A moderately easy day hike in the Lost Pines of Texas
General location: About twelve miles east of Bastrop
Length: About 7.8 miles round trip
Elevation: 370-500 feet
Maps: Buescher State Park hiking trail map, Smithville 7.5-minute USGS quad
Best season: Fall through spring
Water availability: None
Special attractions: Dense pine forest
Finding the trailhead: Drive about eleven miles east of Bastrop on TX 71 to the junction with FM 153 and TX 95. Follow the signs to Buescher State Park and go left, or north, on FM 153. Turn left at the entrance at about .6 mile. Drive .8 mile past the entrance station on Park Road 1E to the well-marked trailhead on the right.

The hike: Buescher State Park lies about ten miles east of Bastrop State Park, but is much less visited. A very scenic park road, popular with cyclists, connects the two parks. It lies on the edge of the Lost Pines area of Texas. The isolated patch

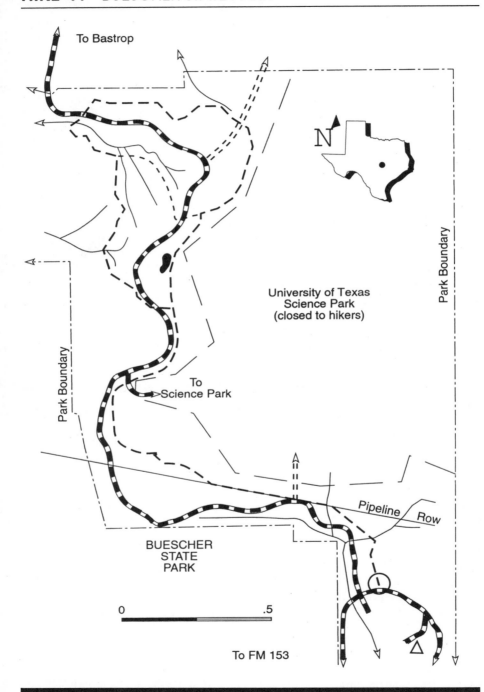

To Bastrop

University of Texas
Science Park
(closed to hikers)

Park Boundary

Park Boundary

To
Science Park

Pipeline Row

BUESCHER
STATE
PARK

0 .5

To FM 153

of loblolly pines grows about 100 miles west of the vast East Texas pine forests. The park area has a surface layer of sandstone and sandy soil that is conducive to the pines' growth, even though it gets less rain than East Texas.

The trail starts largely in oak-juniper woodland, with only a few scattered pines. Aluminum rectangles and blue plastic triangles on the trees help mark the route. At about .5 mile, it hits a pipeline right-of-way. The trail appears to cross the right-of-way and enter into the woods on the other side, but it doesn't. Go left, or west, on the right-of-way for about .4 mile. Ignore the paved park road that touches the right-of-way on the left and the dirt road that crosses it. The trail reenters the woods on the right at a well-marked point.

The pines become more common as you progress along the trail. At about 1.7 miles, the trail crosses the University of Texas Science Park entrance road where it intersects with the main park road. The trail parallels the park road for the next half mile or so. At about 2.2 miles, you hit the start of the trail loop at a junction. Go right.

A small pond is passed at about 2.5 miles. At about 2.9 miles, you will hit a dirt road and trail intersection. Take the right fork across the road. If you wish to shorten the loop, go left back into the woods, following the signs. At about 3.4 miles, the trail crosses a gravel county road. The trail enters a scenic ravine with tall pines. At about 4.2 miles, the trail crosses the main park road and enters into another ravine. At about 4.6 miles, in a ravine, the trail forks. Go right and climb up a low ridge and back down into a broad ravine. The small valley is heavily wooded with pines and even has a small footbridge over the intermittent creek. At about 5.6 miles, you recross the main park road. On the other side of the road, you hit the first trail junction, the starting point for the loop. Go right and retrace the first 2.2 miles back to the trailhead.

Insects can be a nuisance, especially in spring and summer. Summers are usually hot and humid. If you leave the trail, be careful not to get lost in the dense woods. The Buescher trail is usually considerably less busy than the Lost Pines Trail in nearby Bastrop State Park but has more contact with roads. Buescher State Park has great car camping facilities but does not allow back country camping.

HIKE 42: *TOWN LAKE*

General description: An easy day hike around an urban lake
General location: Austin
Length: About 4.5 miles round trip
Elevation: 430-450 feet
Maps: Hike and Bike Trails of Austin (Austin Parks and Recreation Department), Austin West and Austin East 7.5-minute USGS quads
Best season: All year
Water availability: Trailhead, Zilker Park
Special attractions: Lake, accessibility
Finding the trailhead: The Town Lake hike and bike trail has numerous access points. This hike starts from the parking lot on the south side of the lake by the

A footbridge arches over Barton Creek along Town Lake Hike and Bike Trail.

large municipal auditorium. The parking lot lies on the west side of the South First Street bridge between the lake and the auditorium.

The hike: Austin has one of the finest systems of jogging and cycling trails in Texas. Many of the trails follow creek drainages that flow into the Colorado River, now dammed into Town Lake. The city owns most of the property fronting the lake and has turned it into a large park. A long, improved trail was built along much of the lakeshore. The trail covers about 8.5 miles in its entirety, but this hike will follow an easy 4.5-mile loop.

From the suggested starting point by the auditorium, the trail goes west through parkland along the lake, crossing under the railroad and Lamar Boulevard bridges. At the confluence of Barton Creek, the trail crosses an arched steel footbridge over the creek. Side trails continue up Barton Creek, past the Barton Springs Pool and onto the Barton Creek Greenbelt trail (See Hike 39). However, stay on the main trail along the lake. Watch for the enormous bald cypresses below the trail.

At the large MoPac Highway (TX Loop 1) bridge, the trail crosses the lake to the north shore on a footbridge suspended under the MoPac bridge. On the other side, side trails go left to Deep Eddy Pool and straight ahead up the Johnson Creek Greenbelt. Turn right, and continue to follow the lakeshore back to the east.

As the trail continues around the loop, it again crosses under the Lamar and railroad bridges. The trail between the Lamar and MoPac bridges is lined with beautiful redbud trees that bloom in early spring. At Shoal Creek, the trail crosses a small footbridge and a trail turns left, up the long Shoal Creek Greenbelt. Just beyond, the trail passes under the South First Street bridge. Climb the bank up to the bridge and cross back to the south side of the lake and the trailhead.

HIKE 42 *TOWN LAKE*

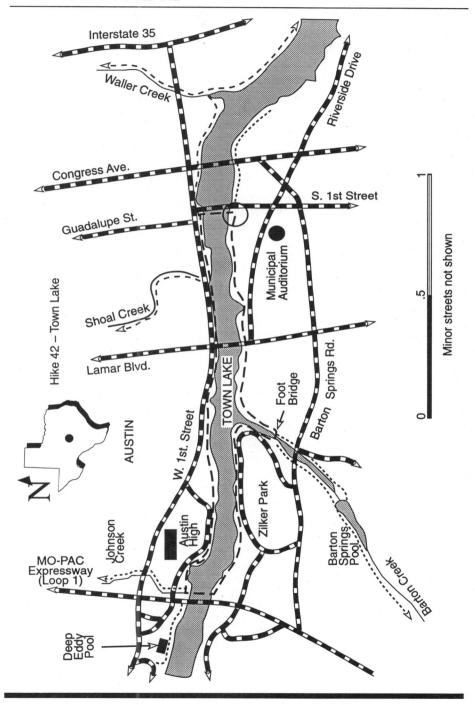

Interstate 35

Waller Creek

Riverside Drive

Congress Ave.

S. 1st Street

Guadalupe St.

Municipal Auditorium

Hike 42 – Town Lake

Shoal Creek

Minor streets not shown

Lamar Blvd.

1

.5

0

TOWN LAKE

Foot Bridge

Barton Springs Rd.

AUSTIN

W. 1st. Street

N

Zilker Park

Johnson Creek

MO-PAC Expressway (Loop 1)

Austin High

Barton Springs Pool

Barton Creek

Deep Eddy Pool

The trail can be followed several miles further east on the north shore to and across Longhorn Dam. The Town Lake trail acts as a nucleus for many of the other Greenbelt trails. My favorites, and the two longest, are the trails up the Barton Creek and Shoal Creek greenbelts. The Town Lake Trail is probably one of the busiest in Texas, with walkers, runners, and cyclists. The trail is beautiful, but don't expect a wilderness experience. Instead, relax and watch the myriad other people. Since the trail is in a city, it probably should be avoided at night, especially the section east of Interstate 35. Incidents are rare, but there's no use tempting fate.

HIKE 43: *PALMETTO*

General description: Two easy adjacent trails in a lush swampland
General location: About ten miles southeast of Luling
Length: About 1.5 miles round trip for both trails
Elevation: 300-315 feet
Maps: Palmetto State Park map, Ottine 7.5-minute USGS quad
Best season: Fall through spring
Water availability: Trailhead
Special attractions: A relict bog leftover from cooler, wetter times
Finding the trailhead: From the center of Luling, take US 183 southeast, past the

HIKE 43 *PALMETTO*

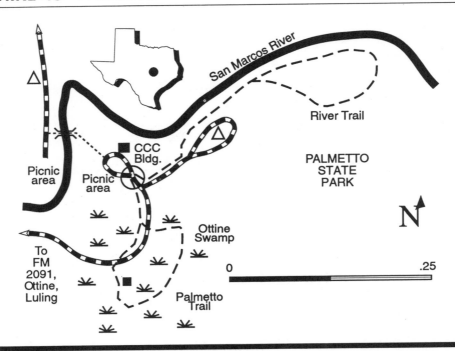

Interstate 10 junction. The Palmetto State Park entrance is on the right at about 6.3 miles. Drive 2.9 miles into the park, through the village of Ottine. Cross the San Marcos River and turn left at the second park road on the left. Drive about .6 mile further through dense woods to the parking area in front of the imposing stone CCC picnic shelter.

The hike: Although this hike is very short and easy, I've included it because Palmetto State Park is one of my favorite places in Texas. The surrounding countryside consists of gentle hills with post oak woodlands and scattered pastures. The San Marcos River has cut a broad valley through the hills. Swamps formed in the floodplain in the park because of flooding and thermal springs. The extra water supports a lush, jungle-like woodland reminiscent of the swamps of the wetter Big Thicket far to the east. Thick stands of dwarf palmetto give the park a tropical look. Unfortunately, heavy ground water usage in the area has caused many of the springs to dry up, shrinking the remaining bog. A CCC-built artesian well provides the remnants with needed water.

For the first trail, walk back up the entrance road about 100 yards to the marked Palmetto Trail on the left. Be sure to pick up one of the nature trail booklets at the trailhead. The trail makes a .3-mile loop through the heart of the Ottine Swamp. Note the sulfur smell of the water flowing from the CCC well. In spring, both native and exotic irises choke the waterways. Palmettos form a dense understory, while a canopy of green ash, cedar elm, and oaks hides the sun. The park seems to be a favorite for armadillos; I've seen at least one on almost every visit.

To reach the second trail, walk 100 yards deeper into the park from your car, following the signs to the campground. The marked River Trail starts on the left across from the bathrooms. The trail follows the river, with the campground on the right initially. Several small side trails meet the main trail, but they either go to the river or back to the campground. When the main trail forks, you can go either way; the trail simply makes a loop. The trail passes through lush forest, although not as swampy as the Palmetto Trail. A booklet picked up at the trailhead will help explain the sites and vegetation along the route. Be sure to note the size of some of the trees along the path, especially the cedar elms and cottonwoods.

HIKE 44: *MATAGORDA ISLAND*

General description: An easy day hike along the beach of a virtually uninhabited barrier island
General location: About eleven miles south of Port O'Connor
Length: Variable; see text
Elevation: Sea level-ten feet
Maps: Matagorda Island State Park map, Pass Cavallo SW and Long Island 7.5-minute USGS quads
Best season: Year-round
Water availability: None

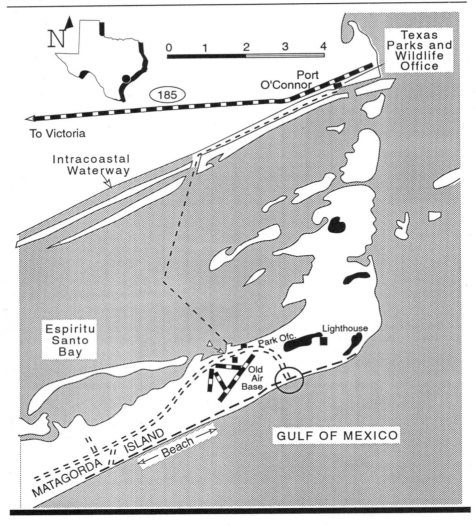

Special attractions: Undeveloped and empty Gulf Coast beach, whooping cranes and other endangered species, prolific bird and animal life

Permit: Required for camping

Finding the trailhead: Matagorda Island has the most unique access of any hike in this guide. There is no causeway or bridge to the island, so a boat is necessary to get to the island. The Texas Parks and Wildlife Department runs a ferry boat to the island on weekends and holidays from the docks in Port O'Connor (on the coast about forty miles southeast of Victoria) for a reasonable fee. On the island they run a shuttle from the docks on Espiritu Santo Bay the short distance across the island to the Gulf beaches. Call the park at (512) 983-2215 before going to check on departure times and dates. Alternatively, boats can be chartered in Port O'Connor.

The hike: Matagorda Island is one of only two barrier islands along the lengthy Texas coast that is not connected to the mainland by a causeway or bridge. Hence, the thirty-eight-mile-long island is almost completely undeveloped. No condos, hotels, fishing cabins, marinas, power lines, or other developments mar its shores. Only a ranch house or two, an 1852-vintage lighthouse, and an abandoned Air Force base now used by the Parks and Wildlife Department occupy the island.

The 56,000-acre island was originally occupied by the Karankawa Indians. Europeans such as Cabeza de Vaca visited the island soon after the white man first appeared in the new world. Eventually, ranching became the primary activity on the island before the state and federal governments acquired the island from private owners. Today Matagorda is managed jointly by the state and federal governments as Matagorda Island State Park and Wildlife Management Area and Matagorda Island National Wildlife Refuge.

The island is famous for its plentiful birdlife. Well over 300 species of birds use the island as a permanent home, winter home, or migration stopover point. Deer and coyotes roam the interior grasslands, while alligators lurk in numerous ponds. Nineteen threatened or endangered species, including the whooping crane, peregrine falcon, and Kemp's Ridley sea turtle, find refuge on Matagorda.

The hike can be of almost any length desired. After arriving at the docks, catch the shuttle over to the other side and hike as far along the beach as your heart desires. The island is a classic Texas barrier island with broad sandy beaches its entire length. Inland from the beach lie dune ridges, flat grassy barrier flats, and finally the fertile marshes lining the bay. Unfortunately, also common to all of

Alligators frequent the lakes and marshes of Aransas National Wildlife Refuge.

the Texas barrier islands, any trash thrown anywhere in or washed into the Gulf of Mexico usually finds its way onto the beaches. It makes for a depressing multi-national mix of garbage.

With the water to cool you off, the island is fun to visit any time of year. Bring plenty of water and food; there is none on the island. Also there is little shade, other than near the docks, so bring sunscreen. Be wary of jellyfish and stingrays on the beach and in the surf. Swim carefully; there are no lifeguards and occasionally undertows can be dangerous. Camping is allowed near the docks and on certain beach areas. Mosquitoes can be vicious inland from the beach, especially in the evening, so come prepared.

All the warnings aside, Matagorda Island makes a great trip. There aren't many places in United States where you can find over thirty-nine miles of undeveloped, almost empty beach. To get around more of the island, consider bringing a mountain bike along to complement the hike.

HIKE 45: ARANSAS

General description: Four short easy hikes at Aransas National Wildlife Refuge
General location: About forty miles northeast of Rockport
Length: About 4.5 miles round trip total for all four trails
Elevation: Sea level to fifty feet
Maps: Aransas National Wildlife Refuge brochure, Tivoli SE and Mesquite Bay 7.5-minute USGS quads
Best season: October through March
Water availability: Refuge headquarters
Special attractions: Whooping cranes, alligators, wildlife
Finding the trailhead: From the center of Rockport, drive north on TX 35 about twenty-three miles to the FM 774 junction. Turn right, following the signs to Aransas National Wildlife Refuge. Follow FM 774 about 9.5 miles to the junction with FM 2040. Turn right on FM 2040 and drive about 6.9 miles to the refuge visitor center.

The hike: Because Aransas National Wildlife Refuge is the primary winter home to the endangered whooping crane, it is probably one of the most famous wildlife refuges in the United States. Because of its location along migratory bird routes and its extensive, rich tidal marshes, Aransas attracts tremendous numbers of birds. Over 350 species have been reported at Aransas, one of the highest counts in the country. Sooner or later, all serious birders show up at Aransas.

The refuge is also home to abundant other wildlife. In the few hours that it took me to hike these trails on a quiet October afternoon, I saw multitudes of alligators and birds, two raccoons, two armadillos, one water moccasin, nine deer, and one nonpoisonous snake devouring an anole. I spent more time observing the wildlife than I did hiking.

Since the refuge trails were so short, I have included all four of the main trails. All have their unique qualities.

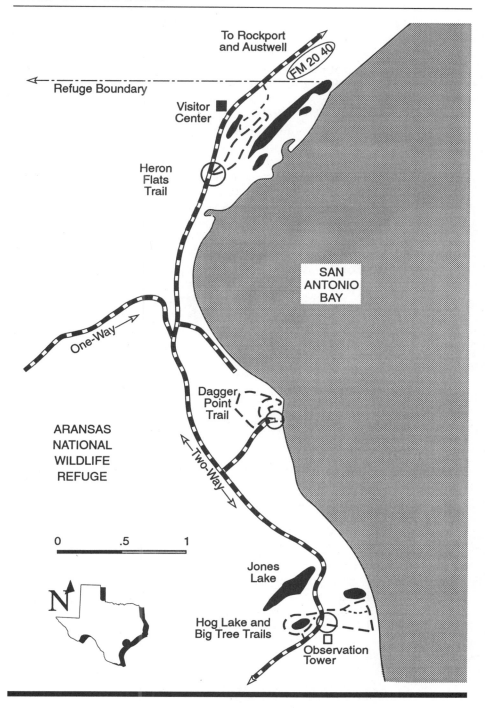

To Rockport
and Austwell

FM. 20 40

Refuge Boundary

Visitor
Center

Heron
Flats
Trail

SAN
ANTONIO
BAY

One-Way

Dagger
Point
Trail

Two-Way

ARANSAS
NATIONAL
WILDLIFE
REFUGE

0   .5   1

N

Jones
Lake

Hog Lake and
Big Tree Trails

Observation
Tower

The first trail, the 1.4-mile-long Heron Flats Trail, lies on the left .5 mile down the refuge road past the visitor center. An elaborate guidebook is available for this trail at the visitor center. Start the trail on the left side of the loop, marked "Entrance." The short "Rail Trail" spur forks left a short way down the trail. The trail passes through oak woods initially, before crossing marshes and following shell ridges to the end of the loop. Many birds congregate in the marshes along the way. Look closely at the pools; alligators are common.

To get to the second hike, the 1.5-mile-long Dagger Point Trail, drive into the refuge about three miles past the visitor center and turn onto the marked side road on the left. Drive .6 mile to the parking lot at the end. One trail a few yards long goes to the shore line. A sign marks the Dagger Point Trail. Two loops are possible, the shorter is only about .5 mile long, the longer is about 1.5 miles long. The Dagger Point Trail quickly reaches the highest point of these hikes when it climbs up onto some old dunes covered with stunted and twisted live oaks and red bays. It then drops down to Dagger Point, a windswept point ideal for enjoying the sunrise or sunset. After the point, you have the option of cutting straight back to the parking lot or continuing with the longer outer loop. Both the short and long loop end on the refuge road. Turn left and walk back to the parking lot.

I've combined the other two trails, Big Tree and Hog Lake, into one 1.5-mile hike. From the visitor center, drive into the refuge about 4.8 miles to the large parking lot at the observation tower. The trail starts by the restrooms. The hike goes left on the boardwalk to the shoreline, but be sure to climb the observation tower. It's one of the best spots to observe the whooping crane and many other birds.

Follow the boardwalk to the shore and turn left. Follow the trail along the shore into the oak woodlands. The trail makes a loop through the woods, passing several very large live oak trees. The largest live oak in Texas grows by Goose Island State Park, between the refuge and Rockport. Continue through the woods to the refuge road. Go left on the road a few yards to the marked Hog Lake parking area on the right. Follow the loop trail around the lake and end up back at the Hog Lake parking lot. A wooden pier extends out into the small marshy lake, making it easier to observe wildlife. Hog Lake and the other smaller ponds along the trail are good places to find alligators. At the end of the loop, just walk right on the refuge road a few yards to the observation tower parking lot.

Mosquito repellent is a necessity most times of year at Aransas. Watch for poisonous snakes and alligators. Don't approach any alligators, even if they are on the trail. They can move quickly over short distances. Don't feed them. Alligators are protective of their young, so don't approach their babies. If you value your pet, consider leaving it at home. This probably goes without saying, but don't swim or wade in refuge waters.

HIKE 46: *PADRE ISLAND*

General description: An easy day hike along a stretch of Padre Island beach
General location: About thirty miles southeast of Corpus Christi
Length: About eight miles round trip
Elevation: Sea level-10 feet
Maps: Padre Island National Seashore brochure, South Bird Island 7.5-minute USGS quad
Best season: All year
Water availability: Malaquite Beach visitor center
Special attractions: Gulf Coast beach, shore birds
Finding the trailhead: From Corpus Christi, take TX 358 southeast across the bay to Padre Island. From the junction of TX 358 (Park Road 22) and TX 361 on the island, go south on TX 358 (Park Road 22) about eleven miles to the North Beach turnoff on the left just before the national seashore entrance station. Drive about .5 mile to the beach and park.

The hike: Padre Island is one of a string of low, sandy barrier islands lining the Texas coast. The island extends south from the visitor center for sixty miles before being cut by the Mansfield Channel at Port Mansfield. A wide, gently sloping beach lines the shore for the island's entire length. Inside of the beach lies a band of dunes, some as tall as thirty or forty feet. Behind the dunes lies a strip of grassland that ends with salt marshes on Laguna Madre. Laguna Madre

Hikers who rise early can watch spectacular sunrises from the shore of Padre Island.

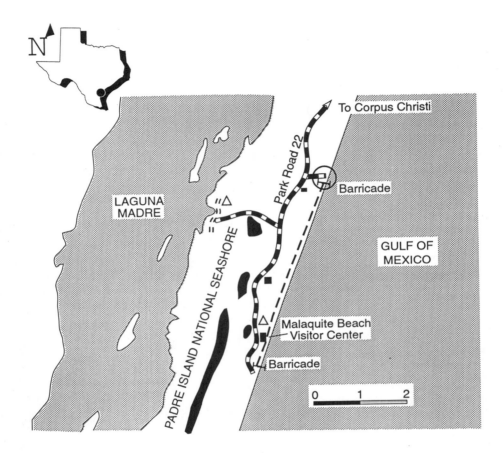

is the very shallow, salty bay that lies between the island and the mainland. Its protected waters are important for birds and fish.

From the end of the road at the beach, hike to the right, south, along the beach. Pass through the barricades that prevent vehicles from driving on this section of beach. The sand near the water is usually firm and easy to walk on. After three miles you will pass the Malaquite Beach visitor center and other facilities on the dunes above the beach. At a little more than four miles you will hit more barricades at the end of the vehicle-restricted beach. Return via the same route. Keep a wary eye open for jellyfish and stingrays on the beach and in the surf.

In summer, this area of beach is extremely popular, so don't come expecting a wilderness experience. However, even though it can be crowded, it's the only part of the island that doesn't allow vehicles on the beach. The island is hot and humid in summer, but just plan to jump in the water to cool off. Remember, there are no lifeguards on most of the beach. On a winter morning you may be surprised at how few people will be out. If you have a four-wheel-drive vehicle, you can leave most of the people behind by driving far to the south along the beach. The hike can also be done in reverse, by parking at the south end of Malaquite Beach.

HIKE 47: *LAGUNA ATASCOSA*

General description: An easy day hike through the brushlands of Laguna Atascosa National Wildlife Refuge
General location: About twenty-five miles east of Harlingen
Length: About 4.5 miles round trip
Elevation: Ten-twenty feet
Maps: Laguna Atascosa National Wildlife Refuge brochure, Laguna Atascosa's Walking Trails brochure, Laguna Atascosa 7.5-minute USGS quad
Best season: October through March
Water availability: None
Special attractions: Birds and animals found nowhere else in the United States
Finding the trailhead: From Brownsville, take FM 1847 about twenty miles north to the intersection with FM 106. From Harlingen, take FM 106 east about nineteen miles to the same intersection. From the intersection, go east on FM 106 about 4.4 miles to the parking area on the right just before a small bridge.

The hike: The 45,000-acre Laguna Atascosa National Wildlife Refuge was established in 1946 to preserve some of the Lower Rio Grande Valley's rapidly shrinking wildlife habitat. Today, with rapid urbanization and extensive agriculture, less than five percent of the valley's natural habitat remains. The small remnants harbor many birds and animals found nowhere else in the United States, such as the ocelot, jaguarundi, green jay, chachalaca, and Harris' hawk. Because of habitat loss, some of these creatures are very rare and endangered. In addition to the unique species, the wildlife refuge's location along migration routes gives it a very high bird count among more common species.

The refuge occupies low-lying coastal plain fronting the Laguna Madre, the long, shallow bay between Padre Island and the mainland. The habitat in the refuge ranges from salt marshes and estuaries to brushland vegetated with mesquite, ebony, prickly pear, huisache, yucca, retama, and granjeno. This hike makes an easy loop through a brushland area of the refuge.

Like most refuge trails, this one follows a service road closed to vehicles. Go through the gate to an immediate fork and go left onto the "Cayo Fork." The right fork is the return leg of the loop. The left fork follows the shallow drainage of the Cayo Atascoso for a little more than two miles. It may or may not have water in it. A pond at about two miles can often hold waterfowl. At two-plus miles the trail cuts sharply right into the brush and away from the Cayo Atascoso. A faint spur road continues south along the Cayo for a short distance.

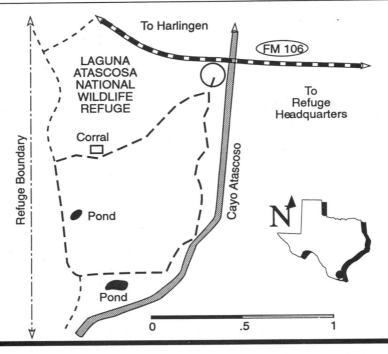

The trail loops back north through the brushland to the first fork and the trailhead. Along the way, you will pass a small pond on the right and a corral on the left. Another faint road forks to the left after the small pond. Ignore it unless you wish to extend the hike.

This is an extremely hot and humid hike in the summer and not recommended at that time of year. The refuge has a number of other trails, making it one of the best areas in the valley for hiking. Most are short, but the loop around Laguna Atascosa itself is on the order of fifteen miles.

HIKE 48: *SANTA ANA*

General description: An easy day hike through the native woodlands of the Rio Grande floodplain

General location: About fifteen miles southeast of McAllen

Length: About three miles round trip

Elevation: 85-100 feet

Maps: Santa Ana National Wildlife Refuge map, Las Milpas 7.5-minute USGS quad

Best season: October through March

Water availability: Trailhead

Special attractions: Native Rio Grande Valley woodland, unique wildlife

Finding the trailhead: From the intersection of US 83 and US 281 in Pharr (just east of McAllen on US 83), go south on US 281 about 8.1 miles to the point where US 281 turns abruptly east. Go east on US 281 about another 4.1 miles to the signed entrance to Santa Ana National Wildlife Refuge on the right. Park at the visitor center.

The hike: Santa Ana National Wildlife Refuge preserves a small remnant of the woodlands that once lined the Rio Grande for many miles. The forests along both sides of the Rio Grande once harbored animals as exotic as the jaguar. Extensive agriculture and urbanization have all but eliminated the subtropical woodland from the Rio Grande Valley on both sides of the border. Today a few pockets of remaining natural habitat provide a last refuge for endangered species such as the ocelot and jaguarundi. Because of the proximity to Mexico and the subtropical climate, a number of birds are found at Santa Ana and other Rio Grande Valley sites that occur nowhere else in the United States. People flock to the refuge hoping to see such rarities as the chachalaca, kiskadee flycatcher, Harris' hawk, and green jay.

The trail starts from the breezeway in the middle of the visitor center. The trail climbs over the Rio Grande levee and descends into dense, scrubby woodland, a startling contrast to the endless cultivated fields surrounding the refuge. At the multiple junction across the levee, go right onto the "B" loop, or Santa Ana's Communities Trail. Ignore the marked Terrace Trail that forks right after a short

HIKE 48   SANTA ANA

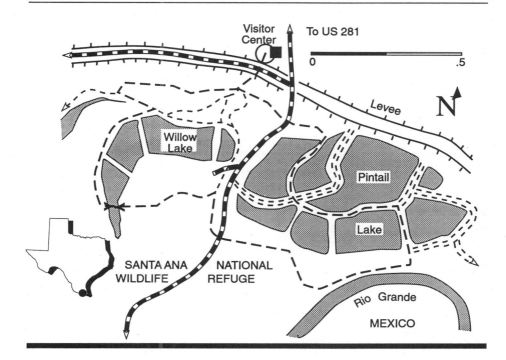

Spanish moss lends a mysterious atmosphere to parts of Santa Ana National Wildlife Refuge.

distance. The trail then winds around shallow Willow Lake through dense forest. Cattails dot the surface of the small lake and waterfowl favor its protected waters. Spanish moss, some of the thickest I've seen in Texas, drapes the woods, creating a mysterious, primeval atmosphere.

On the far side of the lake, just past a photo blind, the trail intersects the "C" loop, the Wildlife Management Trail. Go right, onto the "C" loop. After crossing the paved refuge road, the trail enters an area of more open and scrubby woods. It follows the high bank of the Rio Grande for a short distance before turning north to Pintail Lake. The lake is divided into several different ponds. Several possible trails fork off at the lake, but the main trail is well marked. Finally, the trail recrosses the paved refuge road and ends its loop at the multiple junction just across the levee from the visitor center.

The refuge is very hot and humid in summer and not very pleasant then. During the rest of the year, Santa Ana is a wonderful escape (and one of the few available) from the human-dominated landscape of the Lower Rio Grande Valley. Be sure to explore some of the other refuge trails during your visit.

HIKE 49: *BENTSEN-RIO GRANDE*

General description: An easy day hike along two trails in Bentsen-Rio Grande State Park
General location: About five miles southwest of Mission
Length: About 2.8 miles round trip for both trails
Elevation: 100-115 feet
Maps: Bentsen-Rio Grande State Park map, La Joya 7.5-minute USGS quad

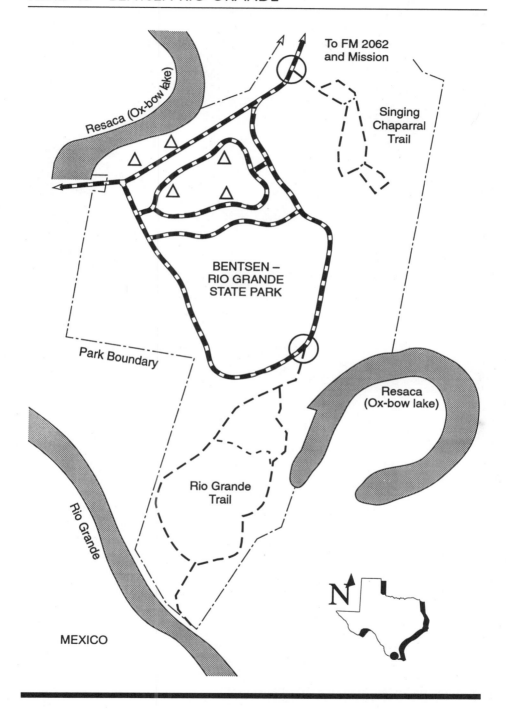

Resaca (Ox-bow lake)

To FM 2062
and Mission

Singing
Chaparral
Trail

BENTSEN –
RIO GRANDE
STATE PARK

Resaca
(Ox-bow lake)

Park Boundary

Rio Grande
Trail

Rio Grande

MEXICO

N

Prickly pears grow to an impressive size in South Texas.

Best season: October through March
Water availability: Park facilities near trailheads
Special attractions: Native subtropical woodland, unique wildlife
Finding the trailhead: From US 83 on the west side of Mission, exit onto TX Loop 374 West. Go west on Loop 374 about 1.5 miles to FM 2062. Turn left and follow FM 2062 about 2.7 miles to the Bentsen-Rio Grande State Park entrance. To get to the Rio Grande Trail, drive .5 mile into the park to a fork. Go left and drive .4 mile to a second fork. Go left again and drive another .5 mile to the marked trailhead on the left. To get to the Singing Chaparral Trail, drive into the park .3 mile from the entrance to the marked trailhead on the left.

The hike: Bentsen-Rio Grande State Park is one of the few public natural areas in Lower Rio Grande Valley. The vast majority of the natural habitat has been lost to the agriculture and urbanization of an exploding population. The native subtropical woodland and brushland of the park provides a small piece of habitat for the area's remaining unique wildlife. Birds (and birders) flock to the park and the valley's wildlife refuges, particularly during spring migration. A number of species are found nowhere else in the United States.

These two short trails wind through the native brush and woodland of the park. Both are nature trails with booklets available at park headquarters. The first hike, the Rio Grande Trail, passes through woods and brush on its way to the banks of the river. It forks just after the start and begins a loop. Go left. Some faint forks to the left along the way drop down to a resaca, or oxbow lake. The park maps show a shortcut loop forking right, but it wasn't very obvious on the ground.

Right after the main trail drops down a bank, it forks. Go left and take the short one-way spur to the river. A stone's throw away lies Mexico. It becomes obvious that the river is little more than a political line on the map as a boundary. It doesn't prevent much of an obstacle to the drug trade, illegal aliens, wildlife, or anything else.

Return from the river to the fork and continue around the main loop and back to the trailhead.

The Singing Chaparral Trail is another easy loop, with two shortcut loops. The nature trail guidebook is particularly interesting along this trail. Just go left at every junction to follow the entire outer loop. The trail passes through one particularly dense patch of woods heavily draped with Spanish moss. The woodland along both trails is suffering, with many dead trees in evidence. With the construction of Falcon Lake upstream on the Rio Grande, the river is no longer allowed to flood. The water from the regular floods was essential to the survival of the woodlands along the Rio Grande. Not only has little woodland been left by man's activities, the tiny remnants are suffering from a human-enforced drought.

HIKE 50: *HAMILTON POOL*

General description: An easy day hike along a cypress-lined creek in the Hill Country
General location: About thirty miles west of Austin
Length: About two miles round trip
Elevation: 700-850 feet
Maps: Hamilton Pool brochure, Hammetts Crossing 7.5-minute USGS quad
Best season: All year
Water availability: Hamilton Creek
Special attractions: Cypresses, collapsed grotto with swimming hole
Finding the trailhead: From the TX 71/US 290 junction on the southwest side of Austin, take TX 71 west about 8.5 miles to the marked Hamilton Pool Road/RM 3238 junction. Turn left and follow Hamilton Pool Road about thirteen miles to the marked entrance to Hamilton Pool on the right. Park in the lot.

The hike: Hamilton Pool is a large collapsed grotto in Hamilton Creek that has filled with water. A forty-five-foot waterfall feeds it from above. Downstream from the pool the creek winds through a small narrow canyon lined with bald cypresses. The high walls help protect the creek from wind and sun and provide a moist environment within which maidenhair ferns, columbine, and mosses

A forty-five foot water plunges into Hamilton Pool in the Texas Hill Country.

thrive. The park is managed by the Travis County Public Improvements and Transportation Department.

From the parking lot, the well-marked trail drops steeply down to Hamilton Creek. At the well-marked junction at the bottom, go left on the Canyon Trail. The path winds along the south bank of the creek for about .7 mile to the confluence with the Pedernales River. Return via the same route to the junction and hike upstream to the pool.

The large grotto with its waterfall and turquoise green pool is impressive. Cliff swallows nest high up on the overhanging cliffs surrounding the grotto. Ferns sprout from seeps in the walls. If it's hot and you have shorts or a swimsuit, jump into the water. Supposedly, the pool is as much as twenty-five feet deep.

Hamilton Pool is not undiscovered, so stay away on summer weekends and you'll avoid most of the crowds. During other times of the year, especially on

124

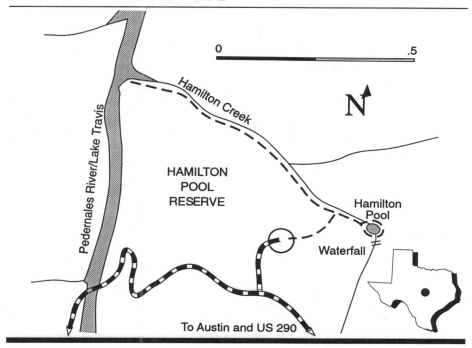

weekdays, you may see no one at all. In late October and early November, the cypresses turn burnt orange, making the creek especially scenic.

If you take water from the creek, purify it, especially if people have been swimming in the pool. On this short a hike I recommend that you carry what you need. Because the pool is heavily visited, be sure to stay on the trail to avoid trampling the delicate vegetation. Park hours are generally 9am-6pm daily.

Summers are hot at Hamilton Pool, but the swimming hole and shady creek make this a year round hike. It's short, but it's one of the scenic jewels of the Hill Country.

HIKE 51: *MERIDIAN*

General description: Two easy day hikes in Meridian State Park
General location: About three miles west of Meridian
Length: About four miles round-trip total for both trails
Elevation: 960-1,060 feet
Maps: Meridian State Park map, Meridian 7.5-minute USGS quad
Best season: Fall through spring
Water availability: Bosque trailhead
Special attractions: Lake
Finding the trailhead: From the junction of TX 6 and TX 22 in Meridian, go west

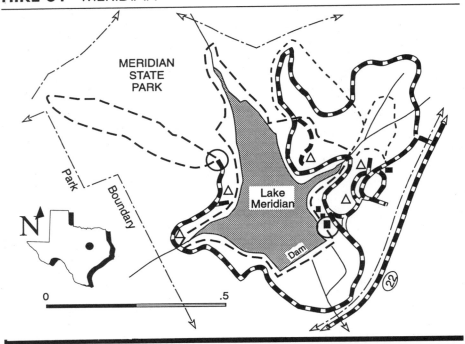

on TX 22 for 2.6 miles to Meridian State Park on the right. For the Bosque Trail, drive into the park about .3 mile to an unmarked junction above the small park lake. Park in the lot in front of the large stone CCC building on the lake below the junction. For the Shinnery Ridge trail, go left at the unmarked junction and drive around the lake about 1.3 miles on a winding narrow paved road. Use care on the road. Park at the circle at the end of the road.

The hike: Meridian State Park is a little-known state park about fifty miles northwest of Waco. The park lies in rolling hills wooded with Ashe juniper and oak. A small lake lies in the middle of the park, created by the CCC when they dammed Bee Creek. The park has two main hiking trails, both of which are described here.

The first hike, the Bosque Trail, starts from the CCC building. Basically, it circles the lake. Follow the lakeshore to the dam, and cross it to the other side. Go right, above the lake, on the other side. Watch out for occasional patches of poison ivy. After about .5 mile, the trail joins the road for a short distance. Go right on the road, across a small bridge. After the bridge, leave the road. Walk through campsite number twenty-four and back onto the trail by the lake. Pass through two campsites on the lake in another .25 mile. The lakeshore forest is dense with oak, pecan, cedar elm, cottonwood, hackberry, and other trees.

A footbridge crosses the creek that feeds the upper end of the lake at a little more than 1.25 miles. At about 1.75 miles, the trail climbs up onto a large

An attractive CCC building rests on the shore of Lake Meridian.

limestone shelf overlooking the lake; this shelf is called Bee Ledge. Several trails lead from the ledge to the park road just above. At the road, there is a road junction. Take the side road into the group campground for about one hundred yards to a trail sign on the left. Take the trail a short distance to a junction. Go right at the signed junction on the Bosque Trail and down into a creek bottom. Go right at the trail junction in the creek bottom. Just down the creek, cross the road and walk through campsite number twenty-seven and back onto the trail. In short order, you will pass some screened shelters and be back at the start.

The slightly shorter Shinnery Ridge Trail starts at the other trailhead described above. A sign indicates the start of the trail at the parking area. Most of the trail winds through dense juniper forest on relatively level ground. There are several benches and trail signs along the way. After about a mile, the trail runs into an old gravel road. Turn right and follow the old road back to the trailhead. To the left, the gravel road ends in fifty yards or so. The park map shows a cutoff trail that would make the loop even shorter, but I did not see it.

Although relatively shady, the trails are very hot in summer. The Bosque Trail can be enlarged slightly by adding the two nature trail loops on the northeast side of the park. Meridian must provide good armadillo habitat. I saw several while hiking these two trails.

HIKE 52: *DINOSAUR VALLEY*

General description: An easy day hike through the hills above the Paluxy River
General location: About sixty miles southwest of Fort Worth
Length: About 4.3 miles round trip
Elevation: 650-850 feet
Maps: Dinosaur Valley State Park map, Hill City and Glen Rose West 7.5-minute USGS quads
Best season: Fall through spring
Water availability: Campground near trailhead

HIKE 52 *DINOSAUR VALLEY*

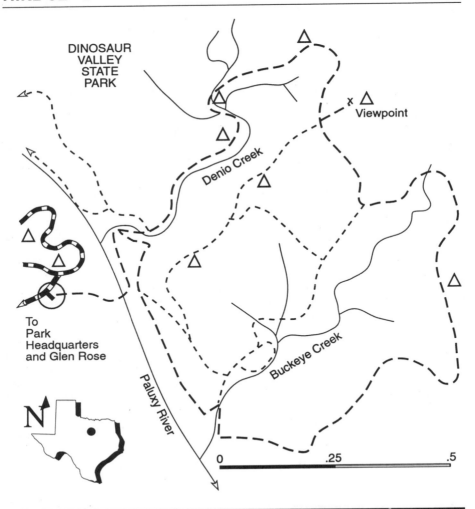

DINOSAUR
VALLEY
STATE
PARK

x Viewpoint

Denio Creek

To
Park
Headquarters
and Glen Rose

Paluxy River

Buckeye Creek

N

0   .25   .5

Dinosaurs left their tracks in the bed of the Paluxy River.

Special attractions: Dinosaur tracks, views
Permit: Required for camping
Finding the trailhead: Drive about a mile west of Glen Rose on US 67. Turn right on Park Road 59/FM 205, following signs to Dinosaur Valley State Park. Go about three miles to the Park Road turnoff on the right. Enter the park and go right at the first fork (to the campground) at about .7 mile. Go right again after another .1 mile. The marked trailhead is on the right after a second .1 mile.

The hike: About 105 million years ago dinosaurs roamed the shores of ancient Cretaceous seas, leaving their footprints in soft, limey mud. Over time, the footprints were buried and hardened into limestone. The Paluxy River has eroded away the overlying layers and exposed the tracks. Three types of tracks occur in the park: a carnivore related to the Tyrannosaurus rex, an enormous herbivore related to the Apatosaurus (formerly called the Brontosaurus), and a third less well identified type of reptile.

The tracks lie in the river bottom upstream from where this hike crosses the river. Be sure to take the time to look at the tracks before or after the hike. Most of the hike travels through the high wooded bluffs across the river from the trailhead. Several loops are possible in the Cedar Brake Trail system; I chose the outer, longest loop. The different sections of trail were marked with different colors (white, blue, and yellow) by the park staff. The outer loop follows the "white" trail.

The trail goes down to the river and crosses it. If you can't find it on the other side, go upstream a bit. Follow the white trail, marked with paint spots on rocks and trees and white plastic triangles. To follow it counter-clockwise, turn right at every junction except on a "blue" trail forking right near the end of the loop.

About two-thirds of the way around the loop, be sure to take the .1-mile "blue" side trail to a viewpoint overlooking much of the park. When the trail drops down into Denio Creek, the route isn't as clear because flooding erases signs of the trail. Go left down the creek and the trail quickly becomes obvious again. The upland areas are wooded most heavily with juniper. The creek bottoms are more lushly wooded with oaks, cedar elms, and other trees.

The trail is hot in summer but bearable with an early start. Plan to jump in the river after your hike.

HIKE 53: *LAKE MINERAL WELLS*

General description: An easy day hike in the cross-timbers back country of Lake Mineral Wells State Park
General location: About three miles east of Mineral Wells
Length: About five miles round trip
Elevation: 900-950 feet
Maps: Lake Mineral Wells State Park map, Mineral Wells East 7.5-minute USGS quad
Best season: Fall through spring
Water availability: Trailhead
Special attractions: Cross-timbers vegetation, rock climbing
Permit: Required for camping
Finding the trailhead: From Mineral Wells go east on US 180 about three miles (or west about fifteen miles from Weatherford) to the marked park entrance on the north side of the road. Drive into the park about .7 mile to a junction past headquarters. Turn left, toward the camping area, and go .8 mile on the main road to a second junction. Go left again, toward the hiking trail and equestrian camping area. Drive about one mile to the end of the road by the equestrian camping area. A sign, "Cross-Timbers Equestrian Trail", marks the trailhead.

The hike: While most of the park activity centers around the lake, an extensive trail system serves both hikers and horses. Lake Mineral Wells lies in an area of north Texas known as the Cross-timbers. The area is typified by rolling hills with scattered rocky bluffs. A dense scrubby forest of oaks and cedar elms cloaks the slopes. A reddish, iron-rich soil is common in the area.

At the trailhead, ignore the large equestrian trail sign and look to its right. A smaller sign saying "Primitive Camping Trail" marks the proper route. The first part of the trail is steep and rocky as it goes up and down the bluffs above the lake. Watch for poison ivy. The hiking trail crosses the horse trail in about .5 mile and then again in about another .25 mile. At about one mile, the trail hits a junction with two old roads. Don't turn right or left; continue in the same direction, north, onto the combined horse and hiking trail. At about 1.5 miles the marked hiking trail turns off to the left. At about two miles, it crosses an overgrown paved road and ends shortly at the primitive camping area. Pass the "A" camp area on the left and continue into the "B" camp area.

If you are good at route-finding, follow the trail through the camp area and

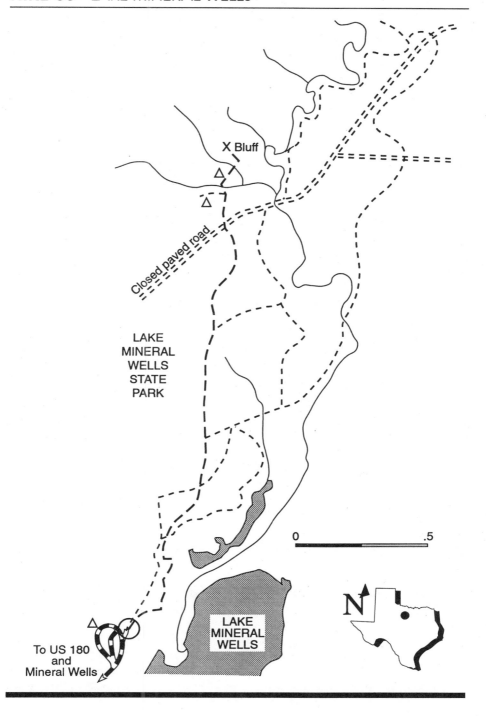

X Bluff

Closed paved road

LAKE
MINERAL
WELLS
STATE
PARK

0   .5

To US 180
and
Mineral Wells

LAKE
MINERAL
WELLS

N

climb an unofficial route up to the top of the bluff above. The bluff offers good views of the valley and the route hiked. Surprisingly, the lake is not visible. Be careful not to get lost climbing back down to the camp area.

The park is very hot in summer and much of the trail is in the open. The return hike can be varied by following the horse trail rather than the hiking trail. The hike can also be lengthened considerably by following the outer part of the horse trail loop.

While you are in the park, be sure to try the much shorter hike on the far side of the lake. It traverses the most interesting part of the park. The rocky bluff above the lake has eroded into high sheer-walled faces with narrow winding canyons, cracks, and caves. The cliffs of firm conglomerate rock have become a favorite of Dallas-area rock climbers. Large cedar elms and other trees thrive in the protected canyons under the bluff.

HIKE 54: *GRAPEVINE LAKE*

General description: A moderate day hike along the shores of Grapevine Lake
General location: About ten miles north of Dallas-Fort Worth Airport
Length: About fourteen miles round trip
Elevation: 535-600 feet
Maps: Northshore Trail of Grapevine Lake map (Army Corps of Engineers), Grapevine and Lewisville West 7.5-minute USGS quads
Best season: Fall through spring
Water availability: Trailhead, Murrell Park, end of trail
Special attractions: Lakeshore views, natural area in urban setting
Finding the trailhead: Go to the Army Corps of Engineers headquarters and visitor center at the corner of TX 26 and FM 2499 (Fairway Drive) a few miles north of the Dallas-Fort Worth Airport. Drive north on FM 2499 about 2.6 miles to Rockledge Park on the left. Drive into the park, turning right at all the picnic area forks. Park at the end of the road at some picnic shelters on the lake after driving about .4 mile.

The hike: This popular trail provides an easy escape for residents of the Dallas-Fort Worth area. Use of a car shuttle halves the hike distance to seven miles. The trail is not perfect; because of the large urban population surrounding the area, litter and boat and car noise occasionally intrude. Still, as the trail passes from dense patches of oak, cedar elm, and hackberry to open views of the lake, it's hard not to enjoy the hike.

The trail crosses several park roads over its seven miles, but is well-worn and easy to follow. From the parking area at Rockledge Park, follow the obvious trail winding northwest along the lakeshore. The trail generally passes through woods except when right on the lakeshore. The trail has some very slight ups and downs as it crosses hilly ridges and creeks.

At a little less than two miles the trail passes through an old abandoned picnic area, a good lunch stop. Between about three and four miles the trail follows an old, closed asphalt road. The trail then crosses Simmons Road and passes

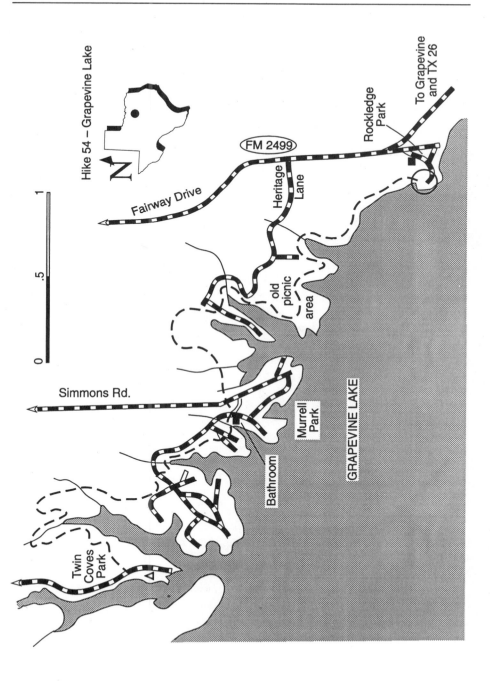

Hike 54 – Grapevine Lake

FM 2499

Fairway Drive

Heritage Lane

Rockledge Park

To Grapevine and TX 26

old picnic area

Simmons Rd.

Murrell Park

Bathroom

GRAPEVINE LAKE

Twin Coves Park

N

1

.5

0

through Murrell Park. Water and restrooms can be found here.

After leaving Murrell Park, the trail winds its way around a large arm of the lake. The last two miles have several short steep hills and pass through dense, shady woods. Watch out for poison ivy if you leave the trail. The trail ends at the entrance of Twin Coves Park and campground. A side trail that forks left just before the end leads to a nature trail at the campground.

Mountain bikes can also use this trail, so expect to see a few. No camping is allowed on the trail, so if you want to camp plan to stay at the developed Twin Coves Park. The Corps of Engineers plans to extend the trail all the way to US 377 eventually. Another trail follows part of the south shore of the lake, adding another possible hike at Grapevine Lake.

HIKE 55: *TRINITY TRAIL*

General description: A moderate day hike along the shores of Lake Lavon
General location: About twenty-five miles northeast of Dallas
Length: About eighteen miles round trip
Elevation: 495-540 feet
Maps: Trinity Trail map (Collin County Public Works, McKinney, TX), Wylie 7.5-minute USGS quad
Best season: Fall through spring
Water availability: Trailhead, Collin Park, trail end
Special attractions: Lake Lavon
Finding the trailhead: Follow US 75 (North Central Expressway) north out of Dallas to the Parker Road-FM 2514 exit (Exit 30) in Plano. Turn right and follow Parker Road east for about 8.8 miles to FM 1378. Turn left on FM 1378 and go 2.4 miles to FM 3286. Turn right and go .8 mile on FM 3286 to County Road 967 (Brockdale Park Road). Turn right and go about 1.8 miles into the park. Stop at the bathroom on the hill just above the boat ramp.

The hike: Lake Lavon, managed by the Army Corps of Engineers, rests in an area of gently rolling grasslands. Here and there patches of woods break up the open terrain, especially along the creeks. The lake is not wilderness—homes, parks, and farms line some of the lakeshore. The parks are popular, especially on weekends, but the trail is surprisingly little used. Equestrian users are probably as common as hikers. The trail makes an easy day trip escape from Dallas. The round trip length is almost eighteen miles, but a car shuttle halves the distance. Even shorter walks are possible by utilizing Collin Park in the middle as a trailhead.

The trail is very faint, especially at first. However, the trail winds along the open lakeshore for most of its distance, making it difficult to get lost, even without the trail. The trail starts through the gap in the fence just to the right of the bathroom. Walk down the slope toward the lake and to the right. The trail isn't always easy to follow, but just continue to work south along the lakeshore as it winds around coves and points. The small creek crossings can be wet and marshy at times, especially in the spring. Occasional trail markers will reassure

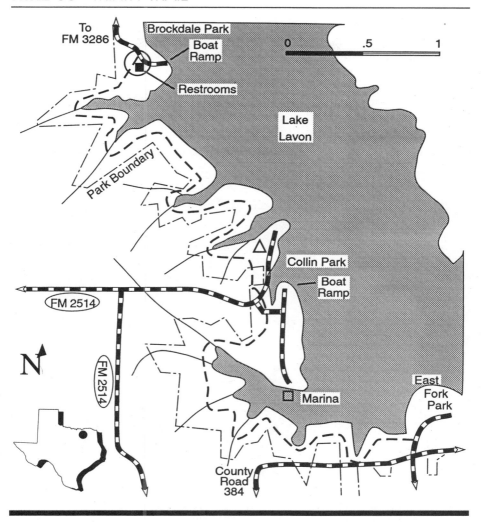

you that you are on the correct route. White painted pipes and fenceposts often mark the places where the trail crosses fences.

The trail reaches Collin Park at about five miles. The approach to the park follows a road past some houses for a short distance just before entering the park. At Collin Park the trail stays well inland from the marina and the point. It then continues winding along the lake for the next four miles to East Fork Park. Just before the end, a right fork leads a short distance up a hill to a parking area on County Road 384. The other fork leads into the park and the end.

HIKE 56: *EISENHOWER*

General description: A relatively easy day hike on the bluffs above Lake Texoma

General location: About seven miles northwest of Denison

Length: About eight miles round trip

Elevation: 620-710 feet

Maps: Eisenhower State Park map, Denison Dam 7.5-minute USGS quad

Best season: Fall through spring

Water availability: Trailhead, campground areas

HIKE 56 *EISENHOWER*

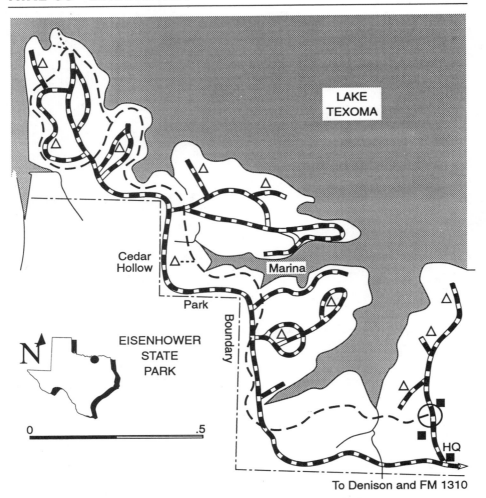

Special attractions: Lake

Finding the trailhead: From Denison, go about five miles northwest on TX 75A to Denison Dam. Turn left on the south side of the dam onto FM 1310 and go 1.9 miles to Eisenhower State Park. Just past the park headquarters, go right at the road fork. The marked trailhead is on the left in a very short distance. A small parking area is on the right.

The hike: Eisenhower State Park was named for President Eisenhower who was born in nearby Denison. The park perches on rocky bluffs that rise out of the waters of Lake Texoma.

Coves cut deeply into the shoreline creating a very irregular coast. Wave action from the large lake (one of the largest in Texas) is rapidly eroding the rocky bluffs. The hike winds its way around the coves and points through thick woods. The trail is not truly wild: it crosses park roads several times and passes several campgrounds. The mileage can be halved with an easy car shuttle within the park.

The trail heads straight into dense woods of oak, cedar elm, ash, and other trees. There are quite a few small ups and downs along the way. Poison ivy grows here and there. Limestone fossils abound in the bedrock.

The trail crosses the first park road in about .75 mile. The trail crosses the road again twice in a row at close to 1.5 miles. A short marked side trail to Cedar Hollow group campground goes left at about two miles. The trail crosses the road again at about 2.5 miles. As the trail circles the next point and the Fossil Ridge campground, numerous side trails cut up to the campsites and down to the lake. The trail forks on the far side of the campground. Go right, toward the picnic area. The trail is hard to follow through the picnic area; just keep circling around the point until you find it again. The trail crosses another road at the Elm Point campground by zig-zagging slightly to the right on the road. Continue to circle around the campground, cross the road again, and wind up at the end of the loop. Follow the same route back to the trailhead.

The trail can be done in summer, but is hot. The campground is pleasant for spending the night before or after the hike.

HIKE 57: *CROSS TIMBERS TRAIL*

General description: A moderate overnight trip along undeveloped southern shoreline of Lake Texoma

General location: About thirty-five miles northwest of Sherman

Length: About eighteen miles round trip

Elevation: 620-740 feet

Maps: Cross Timbers Hiking Trail map (Army Corps of Engineers), Gordonville and Dexter 7.5-minute USGS quads

Best season: Fall through spring

Water availability: Trailhead, Cedar Bayou Resort, Paw Paw Creek Resort, Lake Texoma

Special attractions: Lake

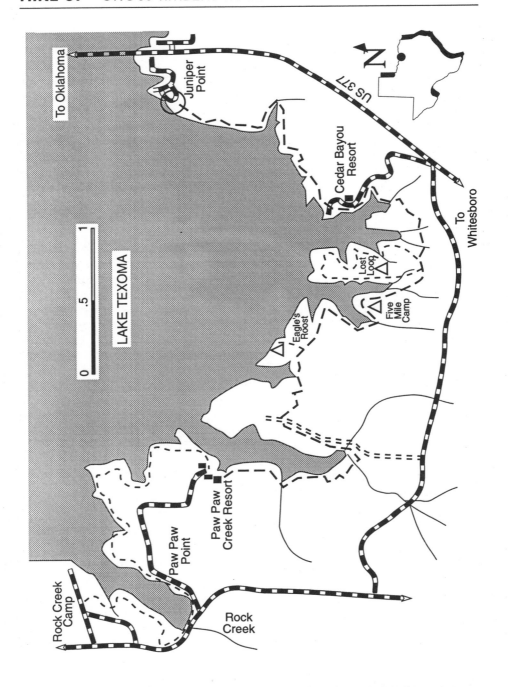

Permit: Required for camping

Finding the trailhead: From the junction of US 377 and US 82 about eighteen miles west of Sherman, go north on US 377 for about 14.7 miles to Juniper Point park. Go left into the western side of the park. At a fork at about .4 mile, go left. The marked trailhead is in a dirt parking lot on the left after about another .1 mile. The last part of the road to the trailhead may be gated closed during slow times of the year. If so, just walk the extra .25 mile on the road.

The hike: The Cross Timbers refers to two belts of timber that stretch north-south across the Texas-Oklahoma line. The soil tends to be thin and sandy, unlike the bordering blackland prairie. A dense scrubby forest of post and blackjack oak, cedar elm, and other trees covers the Cross Timbers country. Washington Irving recounted that his passage through the dense woods was "like struggling through a forest of cast iron." Fortunately the trail makes travel a little easier these days.

The full length of the trail winds along the south shore of Lake Texoma for about fourteen miles. I chose the first nine miles for this hike because the last part of the trail is flatter, less wooded, and more developed. With a car shuttle, the trail makes a good one day hike, otherwise two or more days are generally necessary. Besides the resort areas listed above, water can be obtained from the lake if it's purified.

The 2.5 miles from Juniper Point to Cedar Bayou climbs up and down bluffs above the shore. Heavy erosion from waves on the large lake have cut out the trail in spots. The trail has little net elevation change, but the continuous small, steep ups and downs are more tiring than you would expect. The trail is generally well-marked with orange paint dots, reflectors, and survey tape, and is easy to follow. Occasional mile markers help you locate yourself, although they aren't always placed exactly on the mile.

At Cedar Bayou Resort, walk right past the marina and along the paved entrance road of the resort. The trail cuts back into the woods about 200 yards down the road past the marina behind several campsites on the right. The next stretch of trail leaves the lakeshore for a time and crosses some of the wildest country of the hike. At about four miles, the marked Lost Loop Trail forks right. You can add two miles by taking the loop around a peninsula or stay left on the main trail. One of the primitive campsites lies on the loop. In a short distance the other leg of the loop rejoins the main trail on the right. Stay left. The four-mile marker doesn't quite agree with the location on the Corps of Engineers trail map.

The primitive campsite at Five-Mile Camp lies on the lake and is marked with a "5" sign. Look very carefully for the trail markers just past the Five-Mile Camp. The lake has flooded heavily here, making it a little difficult to find the route for a short distance. At about six miles, the .5-mile side trail to Eagle's Roost Camp takes off to the right. The six-mile marker, however, lies about .5 mile past the turnoff, disagreeing somewhat from the mileage shown on the Corps map.

The trail joins a little-used dirt road at about 6.5 miles. Go left on the road for close to a mile. The trail turns right, back into the woods, about 100 yards past a wooden road bridge. The turn is well-marked. The seven-mile marker is probably located at more like 7.5 miles. Just after crossing Paw Paw Creek at the

The Cross Timbers Trail follows the shore of Lake Texoma.

eight-mile marker, the trail enters poison ivy hell. Up until this point there have been small scattered clumps along the way. Well, someone must have fertilized this patch. The field of Texas-size ivy, as much as four or five feet tall, almost closes the trail. Fortunately, it only lasts for fifty or 100 yards. You may want to carry a bar of soap with you. If you brush some of the noxious plant, cut down to the lake and scrub it off immediately and you should be okay.

About a mile after the ivy patch, the hike ends at the Paw Paw Creek marina and resort. The trail is hot in summer. Except for the occasional cold front in winter, the rest of the year is a more pleasant time to hike. Camping permits can be obtained at the Corps office at Denison Dam near Denison or, from April 1 to October 31, at the Juniper Point park entrance station on the east side of US 377.

HIKE 58: *DAINGERFIELD*

General description: An easy day hike around a small East Texas lake
General location: About forty miles north of Longview
Length: About 2.5 miles round trip
Elevation: 355-530 feet
Maps: Daingerfield State Park map, Daingerfield 7.5-minute USGS quad
Best season: Fall through spring
Water availability: Trailhead, park campgrounds
Special attractions: Lake, dense forest, fall color
Finding the trailhead: From the TX 49/US 259 junction in Daingerfield (about

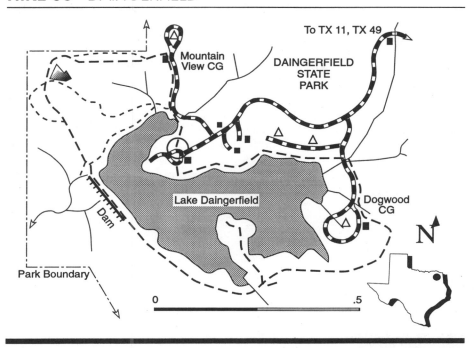

forty miles north of Longview), drive east on TX 49 about 2.5 miles to the marked park entrance road on the right. Drive into the park about 1.2 miles, not turning off anywhere, and park in the large lot at the bathhouse and picnic area above the lake.

The hike: The small, but beautiful, Daingerfield State Park lies in the dense pine-hardwood forests of northeast Texas. The CCC, much of whose work is still in evidence, originally developed the park in the 1930s. Since Daingerfield has been a park for over fifty years, the trees have become quite large.

Although most of Texas does not have notable fall colors, the sweetgums and other trees lining the lake can have good displays some years.

You will notice as you hike along the trail that the soil and rock are reddish-colored. The color is indicative of high iron concentrations in the area. The ore is rich enough to mine near the park and is heavily utilized by Lone Star Steel.

From the bathhouse area, walk down toward the lakeshore to the right, or north, across the mowed grass. At the little side creek, one of the park roads comes close to the lake shore. Follow the road up the hill to the Mountain View Camping Area (sites 29-40). Before you climb the hill you will notice the lakeshore trail going to the left around the lake. Ignore it unless you want to shortcut part of the hike.

At the camping area, follow the obvious trail disappearing into the woods behind the restroom. The trail splits quickly but rejoins in a bit. I recommend the main, or left trail, rather than the one that follows the boundary fence. The trail climbs steadily, reaching a fairly prominent hilltop for East Texas. With less trees, the view to the southwest would be quite impressive. As it is, you'll have to peer through the trees. Stick with the main trail on the hilltop. A less-used trail cuts back east the way you came. Another follows the fence line back down the hill. Regardless, they all end up at the lake.

The main trail drops steeply down the south face of the hill to an unofficial junction in a ravine. The right fork ends very quickly at the creek, so go left, uphill, to the junction with the main lake loop trail. Go right, across the wooden foot bridge onto the dam. After about .5 mile of circling the lake, the trail crosses the neck of a peninsula. Watch carefully and follow the faint spur trail out onto the end of the peninsula for a good view of the lake and park. After leaving the peninsula, continue to circle the lake until you hit the developed Dogwood Camping Area.

A hiking trail circles Lake Daingerfield.

From the campground, go right on the paved park road about 200 yards to the marked continuation of the trail on the left. Follow the trail about another .5 mile along the shore back to the trailhead at the picnic area and bath house.

Summers are hot and humid, but the hike is short enough to be worthwhile even in the heat. October and November are probably the prime times. I had the good fortune to walk the trail on a crisp, still, late October weekday with few other people in the park. Leaves crunched underfoot, the scent of autumn leaves filled the air, and red sweetgums lined the lakeshore. It's about as "fall" as you can get in Texas.

HIKE 59: *CADDO LAKE*

General description: An easy day hike through the woods of Caddo Lake State Park

General location: About seventeen miles northeast of Marshall

Length: About 2.5 miles round trip

Elevation: 170-300 feet

Maps: Caddo Lake State Park brochure, Karnack 7.5-minute USGS quad

Best season: Fall through spring

Water availability: Trailhead

Special attractions: Cypress-dotted lake, CCC buildings

Finding the trailhead: From the junction of TX 43 and US 59 in Marshall, drive

Bald cypresses dot the waters of Caddo Lake, the only natural lake in Texas.

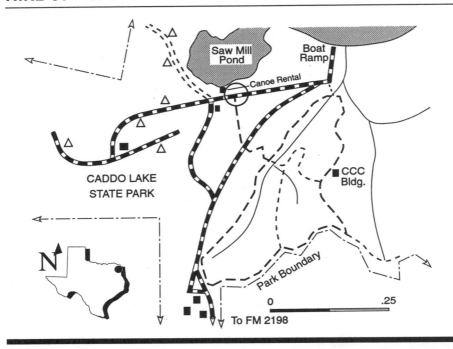

northeast on TX 43 about 15.2 miles to the junction with FM 2198. (Stay with TX 43 through the odd intersection at about 13.5 miles) Go right on FM 2198 about .4 mile to the Caddo Lake State Park entrance on the left. Drive into the park about 1.1 miles to a junction. Go left toward the camping area about .2 mile and park in the lot by the canoe area on Sawmill Pond.

The hike: To me, Caddo Lake is probably the most scenic spot in East Texas. The 32,700-acre lake is the only natural lake in Texas and the second largest in the Southeast. The shallow lake is in reality a maze of mysterious channels and bayous winding through groves of moss-draped bald cypresses. Even with marked routes, many a boater has gotten lost and spent the night in the "Caddo hotel."

According to Caddo Indian legend, the lake was formed by a series of earthquakes and floods. In reality, the lake was formed by a tremendous logjam on the Red River, known as the Great Raft. The incredible jam stretched for over 100 miles downriver. Steamboats found a way around the logjam and upstream across Caddo Lake and the Big Cypress Bayou to found the port of Jefferson. Incredibly, until the Army Corps of Engineers blasted loose the logjam in 1874, Jefferson lagged only Galveston as Texas' biggest port even though it lay over 200 miles inland. Today the lake level is maintained by an artificial dam built in 1914.

The trail starts across the road from the canoe concession on Saw Mill Pond, an arm of the lake and Big Cypress Bayou. The trail climbs low stairs up a hill and crosses a park road and parking area on the hilltop. It then drops down to a junction in a creek bottom. Go right, upstream, following the "Hiking Trail" sign. The trail climbs slowly up to the main paved park road. Go left on the park road a very short distance to an old abandoned road turning left back into the woods. The actual trail parallels the road to the same point, but the foot bridge has collapsed so most people use the road.

Follow the old road along the park boundary fence. At a sharp turn in the fence, the old road forks. Go right, staying with the fence. After maybe 250 yards, follow the route that forks sharply back to the left and leave the fence line road. The old road goes downhill for about 200 yards to another junction. Continue straight rather than turning left. Just downhill from the junction lies a CCC pavilion hidden away in the woods. The old building, solidly built of stone and heavy timbers, is quite a surprise.

From the pavilion, the trail continues steeply downhill to a junction along the creek. The right fork just goes to the road and boat ramp, so turn left and follow the creek upstream to the first junction at the beginning of the loop. Turn right and follow the same route back to the trailhead. The park brochure map is not accurate, with some of the trail segments missing and others marked incorrectly.

Caddo Lake is hot and humid in summer. At the end of October, the cypresses can turn a beautiful burnt orange, making it one of the best times to visit. If you have time, be sure to take a canoe out onto the lake. Nothing else in Texas compares to the experience of paddling through the eerie groves of cypresses. Just don't get lost!

HIKE 60: *FAIRFIELD LAKE*

General description: An easy day hike through woods and fields above Fairfield Lake

General location: About seven miles northeast of Fairfield

Length: About five miles round trip

Elevation: 320-380 feet

Maps: Fairfield Lake State Park map, Young 7.5-minute USGS quad

Best season: Fall through spring

Water availability: Headquarters near trailhead, primitive camping area

Special attractions: Lake, elaborate primitive camp

Permit: Required for camping

Finding the trailhead: From the junction of US 84 and FM 488 in Fairfield, go north on FM 488 about 1.8 miles to the FM 2570 turnoff. Go right on FM 2570 and drive 1.3 miles to the FM 3285/Park Road 64 turnoff. Go about 3.3 miles on FM 3285/Park Road 64 to a turnoff on the left (about fifty yards in front of the Fairfield Lake State Park visitor center) marked with a "Trail" sign. Turn onto the side road and park in the designated lot.

The hike: Fairfield Lake lies in gently rolling hills in the transition zone between the East Texas pine forests and the blackland prairie to the west. The trail passes through woods of post oak, eastern red cedar, elm, white ash, and hickory,

HIKE 60   *FAIRFIELD LAKE*

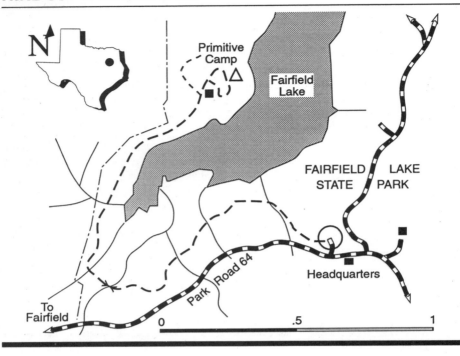

alternating with open grassy fields. Interpretive signs identify many of the trees and other plants on the first half of the trail. A pond and several trailside benches make this an easy, enjoyable hike.

The park map shows the one-way trail length as being about 4.5 miles, but in reality it's only about 2.5 miles at most. The excellent trail winds through woods and fields before reaching the end at the primitive camping area. Primitive is relative. The camp area has flush toilets, water, and charcoal grills. Several winding loops lead to multiple, very private campsites between the bathroom and the lake.

As with most Texas hikes, this one is usually hot and uncomfortable from May through October, but great the rest of the year. With all the amenities, this is a good hike for camping wimps and beginning backpackers.

HIKE 61: *LAKE SOMERVILLE*

General description: An easy day hike through the back country of Lake Somerville State Park
General location: About twenty miles northeast of Giddings
Length: About 8.1 miles round trip
Elevation: 240-270 feet

The Lake Somerville Trailway follows the shore of Lake Somerville for many miles.

Maps: Somerville Trailway map (Lake Somerville State Park), Flag Pond 7.5-minute USGS quad
Best season: Fall through spring
Water availability: Trailhead
Special attractions: Spring wildflowers
Permit: Required for camping
Finding the trailhead: Drive east from Giddings on US 290 about 7.1 miles to FM 180. Turn left onto FM 180 and go 13.7 miles to park headquarters of the Nails Creek Unit of Lake Somerville State Park.

The hike: Lake Somerville State Park lies in gently rolling terrain of mixed open prairie and dense stands of post oak, hickory, blackjack oak, and other trees. The park, located on the shores of Lake Somerville, is divided into two parts, the Nails Creek and Birch Creek Units. A thirteen-mile trail connects the two units. Spurs and side loops create a total of 21.6 miles of trail. Since much of the route is a broad, spacious service road, the park has opened most of the trail to horses and mountain bikes.

Probably the best parking lot is at the headquarters building. Walk into the equestrian camping area just past headquarters. The well-marked trail begins at the back of the camping area. An alternate trailhead is possible a bit further into the park, but the route is somewhat confusing. The broad trail winds through the low hills above Lake Somerville, giving occasional views of the lake. Several small, mowed spur trails turn off, but the main route is obvious.

At about 2.4 miles, the trail forks at a well-marked junction on a hilltop. Turn right onto the hiker-only Flag Pond Trail. The trail passes the Mill Pond primitive camp area and then crosses a bridge over the manmade channel connecting Flag Pond and Lake Somerville. The trail loops around the northeast

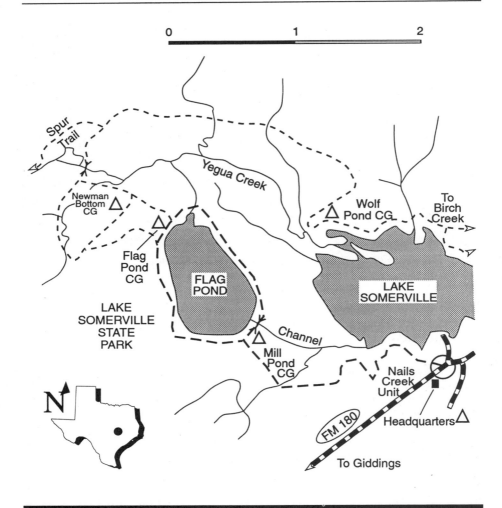

side of Flag Pond on the levee. On the far side of the pond, the trail passes another primitive camp area and two trails forking right. The trail rejoins the main trail at the second fork. Stay left at both forks and continue to loop all the way around Flag Pond to the start of the loop by the Mill Pond camping area. Return to the trailhead by the same route.

If time and energy allow, continue to hike further on the trail. With a car shuttle, the entire main trail makes a long, but excellent, day hike or easier two-day trip. Several primitive camping areas are located along the route. Two of them, Newman Bottom and Wolf Pond, have potable water. Be sure to stop at the side of the trail, well out of the way, if you encounter equestrian users on the trail.

HIKE 62: *FOUR C TRAIL*

General description: A moderate two to three day back pack with a car shuttle through East Texas pine and hardwood forests
General location: About twenty miles east of Crockett
Length: Almost forty miles round trip
Elevation: 200-390 feet
Maps: Four C National Recreation Trail map (Davy Crockett National Forest), Davy Crockett National Forest, Ratcliff, Weches, and Kennard NE 7.5-minute USGS quads
Best season: Fall through spring
Water availability: Trailhead, see text for other sites
Special attractions: Big Slough Wilderness Area, endangered red-cockaded woodpeckers, lush forest
Finding the trailhead: From the junction of TX Loop 304 and TX 7 on the east side of Crockett, go east on TX 7 about 18.4 miles to the marked Ratcliff Lake Recreation Area on the left. Turn in and go about .4 mile to the marked trailhead in the large parking lot on the left.

The hike: Don't panic at the trail length shown above. With a car shuttle, the distance is halved. With the route's multiple trailheads, many hikes of much shorter lengths are possible.

The Four C Trail begins at Ratcliff Lake and ends at Neches Bluff just off TX 21. The trail was named for the Central Coal and Coke Company that logged much of the area's virgin timber early in this century. Almost no virgin forest remains in Texas. Thus, the trail passes through second and third growth forest. White plastic rectangles nailed to trees make the well-maintained trail easy to follow. The trail crosses forest roads numerous times, making many different shorter hikes possible. The trail is usually marked at the road crossings, so by watching closely as you drive down the appropriate forest roads, you should have no trouble finding many different intermediate trailheads. The trail does cross about a mile of private land, so be sure to stay on the trail while crossing that segment.

Over the course of its length, the trail passes through upland forest, bottom-land hardwoods, and swampy sloughs. Much of the trail follows abandoned logging railroad grades, or tramways. Probably the most interesting part of the hike lies in the Big Slough Wilderness Area. The wilderness is one of several small wildernesses tucked away in the East Texas national forests. The Big Slough is a swampy, primeval backwater area adjoining the Neches River. A marked canoe trail also winds through the area. To cross some of the broad, boggy creeks, the trail uses several boardwalks and bridges, one at least 500 feet long. Some of the largest trees of the hike lie within the wilderness area. The Old Tram Loop, marked with signs and blue paint spots, makes a scenic side loop from the main trail in the wilderness.

Neches Bluff, at the north end of the trail, provides views of the Neches River Valley through the pines. Endangered red-cockaded woodpeckers live along

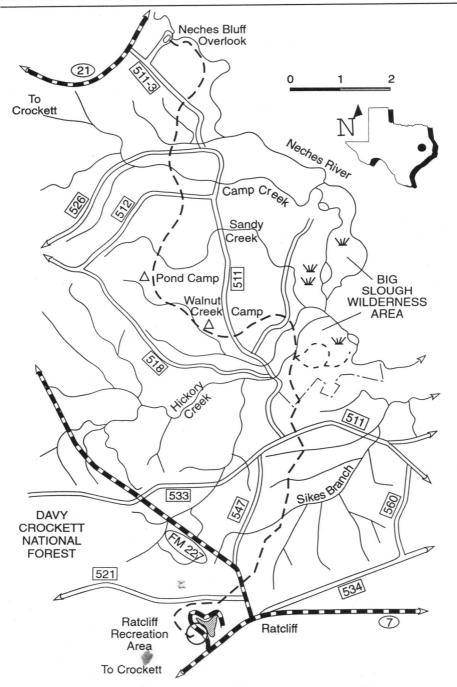

The Four C Trail winds through woodland below Neches Bluff.

the trail's route.

Primitive camping is allowed anywhere within the forest, except during deer hunting season. Ratcliff Lake, at the trailhead, is a developed campground with showers and other amenities. Walnut Creek Camp and Pond Camp lie along the trail. Pond Camp lies on a fishing pond, while Walnut Creek Camp has a pit toilet and an Appalachian-style camp shelter.

Summer is hot, humid, and insect-infested. Poison ivy is common. Short day hikes early in the day are the rule that time of year. Unfortunately much of November and December, one of the best times of year, is deer season. Because of the large numbers of hunters that descend on the East Texas national forests, I don't recommend hiking during deer season. The forest is so busy that the Forest Service doesn't even allow backcountry camping during that period. If you do go then, plan to wear the brightest colored clothing that you can find. Probably the best time for hiking is in late October right before deer season.

Several of the creeks usually have water, especially Hickory Creek in the wilderness area. However, the water is muddy and appears of marginal quality, even with purification. I recommend that you carry all your water.

Don't miss hiking at least part of the Four C Trail. It's one of the premier hikes in East Texas.

HIKE 63: LITTLE LAKE CREEK WILDERNESS

General description: A moderate day hike along the Lone Star Trail into the Little Lake Creek Wilderness
General location: About thirty-five miles northwest of Conroe
Length: About 9.5 miles round trip
Elevation: 230-340 feet
Maps: Guide to Hiking the Lone Star Trail (Sam Houston National Forest), San Jacinto, Richards, and Montgomery 7.5-minute USGS quads
Best season: Fall through spring
Water availability: None reliable
Special attractions: Small East Texas wilderness area, mature forest
Finding the trailhead: From the junction of I-45 and FM 1375 north of Conroe, go west on FM 1375 almost fifteen miles to FM 149. Go right on FM 149 about 1.6 miles and turn left onto a poorly paved road (Forest Road 211) across from FM 1791. Go 2.1 miles—the pavement will end before long—and park at the marked trailhead on the right side of the road.

Foot bridges cross wet areas along the Lone Star Trail.

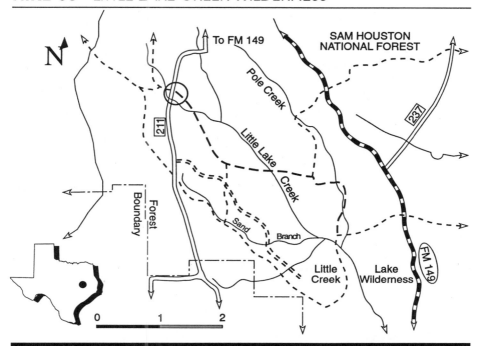

The hike: The Lone Star Trail winds across 140 miles of the Sam Houston National Forest. The trail passes through miles of East Texas pine and hardwood forest. The Little Lake Creek area is one of the wildest and most scenic parts of the trail. Several small areas in the East Texas national forests have been designated as wilderness areas, including Little Lake Creek.

The Lone Star Trail is marked with aluminum rectangles placed vertically on trees. If the rectangle is tilted, the trail turns in the direction of the tilt. Double rectangles indicate a very sharp turn. This section of the Lone Star Trail has not received much maintenance in recent years and has become somewhat over-grown. The main trail is relatively easy to follow, but the loop trails farther into the hike can be difficult to trace. It's best to turn around if the trail fades out; you can get seriously lost in these dense woods.

The first 1.5 miles or so of trail follow an old abandoned pipeline right-of-way and are fairly worn and easy to follow. At a marked junction, go left on the main trail. The right fork (the Sand Branch Trail) looks intriguing, but I haven't followed it. The next stretch of trail (through the wilderness area) gets more overgrown and a little harder to follow, but shouldn't be a problem if care is used. At the next junction, about 3.5 miles, the main trail goes left and the marked Pole Creek Trail goes right to the Little Lake Creek Loop. Unless you are patient and very good at route finding, you should return or continue on the main trail.

Naturally, I chose the Pole Creek Trail. It's confusing right from the start. It makes a very sharp right turn, almost a U-turn, at the sign. Look for the aluminum markers to the right of the Pole Creek sign. The trail quickly enters a jungly old clearcut area and is very difficult to follow. Don't wear shorts on this section of trail. Look closely for the metal markers.

Finally the trail leaves the clear-cut and becomes somewhat easier to follow. It then re-enters the wilderness, marked by a sign and a register in the middle of nowhere. After a little more than 4.5 miles, the trail hits the Little Lake Creek Loop. The left hand route makes a very long loop back to the main trail some miles away. The right hand fork would make an excellent loop back to the trailhead via the Sand Branch Trail mentioned earlier. My original plan was to do the loop, but a short distance down the trail enormous deadfalls completely blocked the path. I tried for a while to find the route through the deadfalls, but was unsuccessful. So I returned the way I came. This part of the wilderness has many old, huge trees making the route-finding hassles worthwhile.

The Forest Service has begun a maintenance program for the Lone Star Trail and its side loops. According to the Forest Service, the first loop just to the northwest of this loop has already been done and may be a better choice for beginning hikers. Supposedly, this loop should be done relatively soon. As with all East Texas hikes, this one is hot and full of insects in summer. Other times of year are better. Also, poison ivy is relatively plentiful, so watch your step. The trail should probably be avoided during deer season.

HIKE 64: *BIG CREEK*

General description: An easy to moderate day hike through the woods along Big Creek

General location: About sixty-five miles north of Houston

Length: About eight miles round trip

Elevation: 280-200 feet

Maps: Guide to Hiking the Lone Star Trail (Sam Houston National Forest), Sam Houston National Forest map, Coldspring and Camilla 7.5-minute USGS quads

Best season: Fall through spring

Water availability: Trailhead, Big Creek

Special attractions: Lush forest, creek, large magnolias

Finding the trailhead: From Shepherd (about sixty miles north of Houston on US 59 or seventeen miles south of Livingston on US 59), go west 11.5 miles on TX 150 to Coldspring. Continue to follow TX 150 out of the other side of town about 1.9 miles to the FM 2025 junction. Go left on FM 2025 about .4 mile to the Double Lake Recreation Area turnoff on the left. Follow the paved Double Lake road (FR 210) to a fork at .6 mile. Go left and follow the road to its end after another .9 mile.

The hike: This hike traverses a particularly scenic stretch of the 140-mile Lone Star Trail. The hike starts at the attractive Double Lake Campground and recreation area. The developed campground makes a good overnight spot before or after your hike.

The trail follows the Double Lake Branch of Big Creek all the way down-stream to the Big Creek Scenic Area. The route passes through lush woods of mixed pines and hardwoods. Several bridges ease crossings of creeks and ravines. As with all of the Lone Star Trail, the route is marked by aluminum rectangles posted on trees. Overall the trail is very easy to follow; in any confusing areas, just look for the aluminum markers. The Lone Star trail guide put out by the Forest Service is helpful.

From the trailhead, walk across the small dam to the four-way trail junction on the other side. Go left, following the sign to the Big Creek Scenic Area. The distances marked on the signs do not always agree exactly but are roughly correct. The trail crosses a power line right-of-way very soon and a dirt road at about .5 mile, but traverses wild country for the rest of the hike.

At about two miles, the trail passes through an area of massive magnolia trees. In early summer, large fragrant creamy-white blooms adorn the branches. At about three miles, the trail enters the scenic area. A sign says "Texas Big Tree Magnolia .5 mile," but we didn't see it. Maybe it died?

At about four miles, the trail hits a well-marked three-way junction and the end of this hike. Don't let it stop you, though. If you have time, go left along the Lone Star Trail and hike along some of the loops in the scenic area. Go right about a mile to reach the scenic area trailhead. If you can set up a car shuttle at the scenic area parking lot, the hike can be turned into an easy one-way five-mile trip.

HIKE 64 *BIG CREEK*

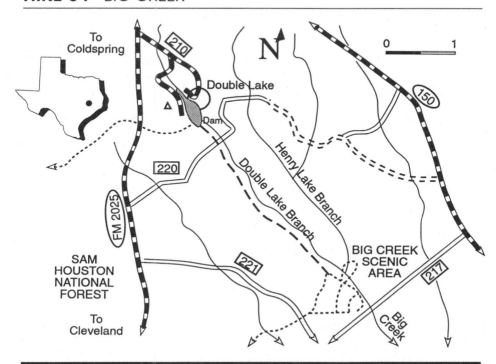

A footbridge crosses the dam at Double Lake along the Lone Star Trail.

The hike can be done any time of year, but as with all East Texas areas, it is usually hot, humid, and mosquito-ridden in the summer. In the warm months, I'd skip the camping and just do the hike, preferably early in the day. In spring, the last mile or two of this hike can be wet and muddy if rains have been heavy. Be careful not to get lost if you stray from the trail. If you like this hike, be sure to follow more of the Lone Star Trail. The trail in this part of the forest is less interrupted by roads than in some other sections. Use great care if you hike during deer season.

HIKE 65: *HUNTSVILLE*

General description: A moderately easy day hike through the woods surrounding Lake Raven
General location: About seven miles south of Huntsville
Length: About eight miles round trip
Elevation: 240-355 feet
Maps: Huntsville State Park Trail Map, Moore Grove and Huntsville 7.5-minute USGS quads
Best season: Fall through spring
Water availability: Trailhead, Lake Raven
Special attractions: Lake, lush forest
Finding the trailhead: Take Interstate 45 about 5.5 miles south of Huntsville and leave the freeway at Exit 109. Follow the signs into Huntsville State Park on Park Road 40. Park at the interpretive center about 1.6 miles into the park.

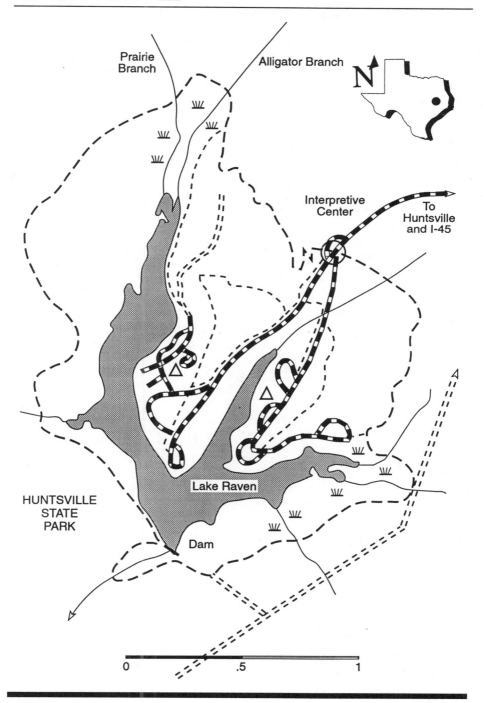

Prairie Branch

Alligator Branch

N

Interpretive Center

To Huntsville and I-45

Lake Raven

HUNTSVILLE STATE PARK

Dam

0   .5   1

The hike: The trail makes a big loop around Lake Raven, the centerpiece of the park. Part of the trail is shared by mountain bikers and several alternate trailheads exist. The trail passes through lush woods of beech, loblolly pine, water oak, and many other trees. Be sure to get the updated trail map at headquarters to help find your way.

Start northwest, behind the interpretive center, on the nature trail. The trail winds initially, but eventually heads northwest. After about a mile, pass the trail forking left that goes back to another trailhead. After the trail crosses the two small creeks of Alligator Branch and Prairie Branch, it turns southwest and passes through an area of upland forest. The trail works its way back to the lake, hitting the dam a little more than halfway around the loop. The trail swings west to cross the creek below the dam.

Shortly after the dam, the trail hits the combined hike/bike loop trail. Turn left onto one side of the loop and continue northeast. After about a mile, the trail joins a dirt road. Go left, across the creek, and fork left again off of the road. The main trail will pass a short left spur that goes only to an alternate trailhead. After

A small waterfall, rare in East Texas, lies deep in the Angelina National Forest.

another mile the hike ends at the starting trailhead.

The hike will usually be hot, humid, and full of insects in summer but is fine if you start early. The trail is easy, but relatively long. Poison ivy is common. If you leave the trail, be careful not to get lost. If you take water from anywhere but trailhead taps, purify it. Be courteous when walking the part of the trail shared with cyclists. The developed campground is attractive for overnight stays. The 140-mile-long Lone Star Trail (see Hikes 63 and 64) passes very near Huntsville State Park. The Texas Parks and Wildlife Department plans to connect the Huntsville hiking trail to it soon.

HIKE 66: SAWMILL TRAIL

General description: A moderate day hike through the lush Angelina National Forest

General location: About twenty-five miles northwest of Jasper

Length: About ten miles round trip

Elevation: 90-150 feet

Maps: Angelina National Forest, Boykin Spring 7.5-minute USGS quad

Best season: Fall through spring

Water availability: Trailhead, Boykin Creek, Neches River

Special attractions: Lush forest, small waterfall

Finding the trailhead: From the junction of US 190 and TX 63 on the west side of Jasper, go about 20.5 miles northwest on TX 63. Turn left on paved Forest Road 313 (marked by a sign for Boykin Springs Recreation Area). Drive south about 2.9 miles to the recreation area. Park in the big day use parking lot along the creek, just below the lake dam. A sign at the parking lot indicates the trail.

The hike: The Angelina National Forest lies in the heart of the East Texas Piney Woods. Tall loblolly pines are mixed in with sweetgums, oaks, and many other hardwoods. The trail travels between two National Forest Service campgrounds, Boykin Springs and Bouton Lake. Like most East Texas trails, this trail crosses relatively level terrain with few elevation changes.

Cross the creek on the wooden footbridge at the parking lot and turn left through the campground. The trail is a bit tricky to follow through the campground. White dots painted on the trees help immensely. Very soon after turning left, the trail crosses the creek again, this time on cemented stepping stones. From the stepping stones, go right, up the wooden stairs. Follow the white dots downstream, across the campground loop road, and into the forest.

The trail follows the creek downstream for over 1.5 miles. Depending on water flow, the creek makes a small waterfall part way down, a rarity in East Texas. The trail also crosses a dirt road at a little more than one mile. The trail forks at a little over 1.5 miles on an abandoned railroad grade. As indicated by the sign, you may take a .75-mile side trip to the left to the sawmill site at Old Aldridge. Otherwise, turn right and continue to Bouton Lake along the old railroad grade. Several bridges and boardwalks make stream crossings easy. A marked, but somewhat overgrown side trail to Blue Hole forks off to the right.

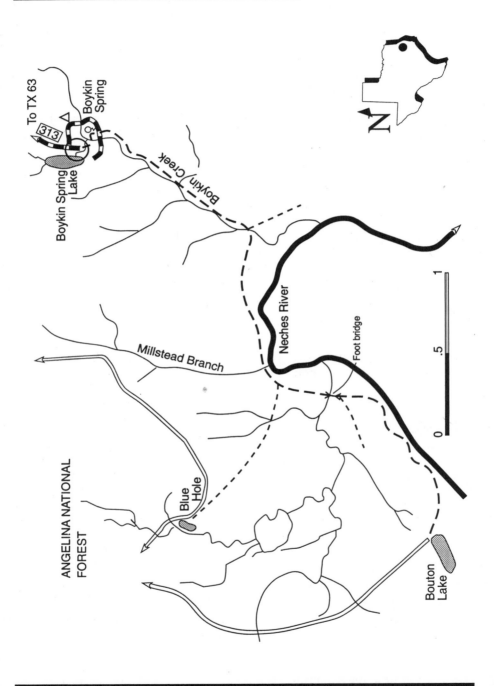

Further on, the small suspension bridge is fun to cross, although the approach steps on one side were missing when I did the hike.

The trail forks on the far side of the suspension bridge. Go left, following the omnipresent white dots, even though it appears less used. The right fork may also lead to Bouton Lake; I don't know since I didn't try it. Much of the last mile follows the banks of the Neches River. The trail ends at Bouton Lake.

Be careful if you leave the trail; it's easy to get lost in the dense woods, especially on cloudy days. Rain is most common in the spring, but take raingear any time of year. Poison ivy can blanket areas of the forest floor, so watch for it. Mosquitoes, heat, and humidity can be miserable in the summer, so plan to hike in other times of year. You may want to avoid the trail during deer season. An easy car shuttle cuts the distance in half. Camping is allowed anywhere in the forest. The trail drains better than some East Texas trails. I did this hike in the midst of a very wet spring and was able to keep my feet dry. The trail is one of my favorites in East Texas, especially in late March when the azaleas and dogwoods are blooming.

HIKE 67: MEMORIAL PARK

General description: An easy day hike in the heart of Houston
General location: Houston
Length: Two to five miles
Elevation: 25-60 feet
Maps: Houston Arboretum and Nature Center trail map, Houston Heights 7.5-minute USGS quad
Best season: Fall through spring
Water availability: Trailhead
Special attractions: Lush woods
Finding the trailhead: The trail lies at the Houston Arboretum and Nature Center at 4501 Woodway Drive. The well-marked entrance is in Memorial Park on the south side of Woodway just east of Interstate Loop 610.

The hike: The Houston Arboretum and Nature Center was established in 1967. The center is part of Memorial Park but is managed by the Houston Arboretum and Botanical Society, a private non-profit educational organization. Unlike the rest of Memorial Park, no jogging or cycling is allowed to help preserve the natural character of the center. The nature center provides a beautiful wooded retreat from the large noisy surrounding city.

A five-mile network of trails criss-crosses the 155-acre center. Rather than describe a specific route, as I do for most of the hikes in this guide, I suggest that you pick up a trail map at the center's office. All the trails are named and well-marked on both the map and the grounds, making it difficult to get lost for any length of time.

The trails wind through a lush second-growth forest of tall loblolly pines and mixed hardwoods. The two-mile outer loop provides a good introduction to the park. Be sure to take the side trail down to Buffalo Bayou in the southeast corner.

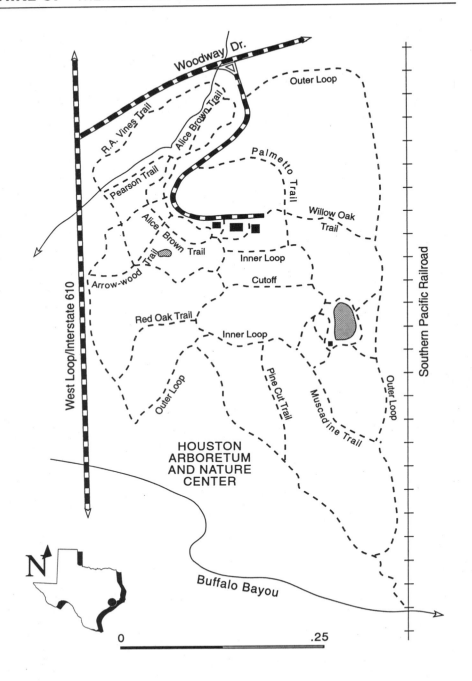

Woodway Dr.

R.A. Vines Trail

Alice Brown Trail

Outer Loop

Pearson Trail

Palmetto Trail

Willow Oak Trail

Alice Brown Trail

Inner Loop

Arrow-wood

Cutoff

Red Oak Trail

Inner Loop

Outer Loop

Pine Cut Trail

Muscadine Trail

Outer Loop

West Loop/Interstate 610

Southern Pacific Railroad

HOUSTON ARBORETUM AND NATURE CENTER

N

Buffalo Bayou

0   .25

When pine beetles killed a patch of pines on the east side, the center planted a native prairie and put in a pond. The pond has the best wildlife, with turtles, birds, frogs, and plentiful chameleon-like anoles. The Alice Brown Trail, an interpretive nature trail, will also be of interest. The nature center provides an oasis of calm in the heart of Houston, but requires little travel to reach. Other trails cross the rest of Memorial Park, but they are more developed and heavily used by joggers.

HIKE 68: *LAKE LIVINGSTON*

General description: An easy day hike through the woods of Lake Livingston State Park
General location: About five miles southwest of Livingston
Length: About four miles round trip
Elevation: 130-150 feet
Maps: Lake Livingston State Park brochure, Blanchard 7.5-minute USGS quad
Best season: Fall through spring
Water availability: Trailhead, campground
Special attractions: Lake, lush woods
Finding the trailhead: From US 59 on the south side of Livingston, take FM 1988 southwest about four miles to FM 3125. Go right on FM 3125 about .5 mile to the Lake Livingston State Park entrance on the left. Drive into the park and stop at the headquarters building.

The hike: The Lake Livingston trail is a nice woodland hike, although not especially wild. It passes through several of the campgrounds and developed areas. The campground makes a good overnight camp area before or after your hike.

Pick up a map at the headquarters before starting your hike. Look at it, then throw it away. Actually, the map shows the trails accurately on the west side of the main north-south park road. Unfortunately, the first part of the hike, to the duck pond and beyond, has numerous errors. In particular, it doesn't show a number of confusing cross trails. I've tried to show most of the trails on the map in this guidebook, but some errors still probably exist. Don't worry if you get confused. The trails lie in a small area of land, so you will find your way to a road sooner or later.

Start the hike from headquarters on the small Oak Flat Nature Trail. The .3-mile trail loops through an area of bottomland hardwoods, before hitting the main hiking trail back near the headquarters. Go right on the main hiking trail. After about another .4 mile, the trail hits one of many cross trails, one of which goes to the duck pond. Rather than list all the junctions, refer to the accompanying map. Overall, try to continue north, before finally turning west and hitting the park road.

Cross the park road and intersect a more improved and built-up trail near the north campground area. The park map does show the western and southern trails much more accurately than it does the area around the duck pond. Follow the trail south through the camping and boating areas. The small southern loop

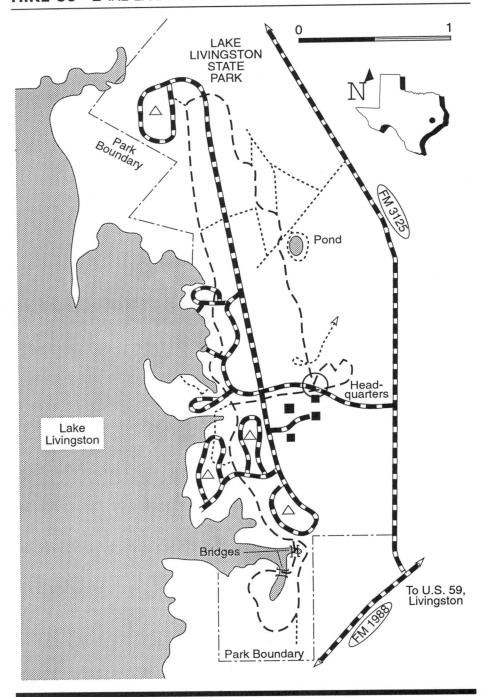

0   1

LAKE
LIVINGSTON
STATE
PARK

N

FM 3125

Park
Boundary

Pond

Head-
quarters

Lake
Livingston

Bridges

To U.S. 59,
Livingston

FM 1988

Park Boundary

becomes wilder and less developed before returning to the heart of the park and the headquarters.

If the park has received a lot of rain, especially in the spring, skip the nature trail and the trails east of the main road. I did the hike after heavy rains and waded almost constantly. The western part of the trail is built-up and will be dry after all but the heaviest rains. Poison ivy is common, so watch out. Getting lost isn't unlikely on a cloudy day on the maze of trails around the duck pond, but you'll soon find your way out in the small park.

HIKE 69: *BRAZOS RIVER*

General description: An easy day hike along part of the Brazos River
General location: About forty-five miles southwest of Houston
Length: About four miles round trip
Elevation: 40-55 feet
Maps: Brazos Bend State Park map, Otey and Thompsons 7.5-minute USGS quads
Best season: Fall through spring
Water availability: Trailhead
Special attractions: Lush forest, red buckeyes in the spring
Finding the trailhead: Drive about 25 miles southwest of the center of Houston on US 59 to FM 2759, just a little short of Richmond. Go southwest on FM 2759 about 1.7 miles to the junction with FM 762. Go straight ahead, south, on FM 762 for about fifteen miles to the Brazos Bend State Park entrance on the left. Drive into the park on the main road for about 3.5 miles to a fork. Go right, following the signs to Hale Lake. Go right again after only about .1 mile and park at about 4.7 miles at the picnic area at Hale Lake. The last stretch of road to Hale Lake is sometimes closed in winter, lengthening the hike somewhat. The marked trailhead is across from the picnic area, just past the group picnic shelter.

The hike: Brazos Bend State Park lies at the confluence of Big Creek and the Brazos River. The coastal plain in which the park lies is very flat, so this hike has very little elevation change. The low, swampy terrain of the park contains many lakes and sloughs. Birds, alligators, and other wildlife thrive in the lush park. Many miles of trails criss-cross the park, more than are covered by this guide. Since many of the trails allow mountain bike use and the park lies near Houston, you will probably see more bikes here than in any other park. Although most of this hike is designated for foot travel only, you will probably see a few cyclists anyway.

The trail starts by passing through a short strip of woods before crossing the paved loop road. On the other side of the road a large sign shows a map of the hiking trail. Part of this hike is not shown on the sign, although it is shown on the park map brochure. Many possible trail loops are possible, but this hike follows the outer loop, so you will turn right at most of the forks. With several intersecting trails, be sure to keep track of where you are on the map.

Take the right fork just past the sign and enter the lush dense woods of oak,

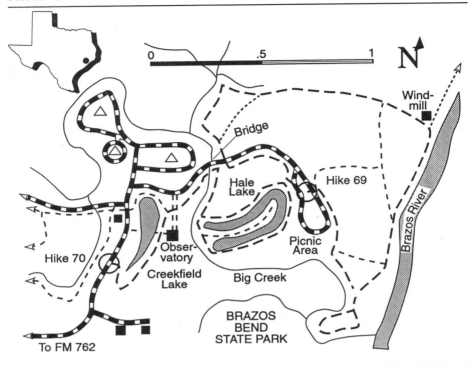

sycamore, hackberry, hickory, cottonwood, sweetgum, and many other species. After about .5 mile, the trail crosses a broad, open pipeline right-of-way and starts the Red Buckeye Loop Trail. Ignore the trail following the right-of-way. The Buckeye Loop circles the peninsula at the confluence of Big Creek and the Brazos River. In March, the shrubby buckeyes bloom scarlet all through this part of the forest. The buckeyes, the narrow winding trail, and the dense woods make this probably the most scenic part of the hike.

A short distance further, the trail forks. Bear right to the next fork in 100 yards. Bear right again onto the loop. After circling the loop, you will return to the same junctions. Bear right again at both forks. The trail will hit the open right-of-way again and a junction. Go straight, along the Brazos River. The trail turns into a two-track dirt road used only by park employees for the rest of the hike.

Bear right again at the next fork onto the marked Brazos River Loop Trail. The Brazos is one of the largest and most important rivers in Texas. The deep muddy river hisses quietly by, down a steep treacherous bank. The headwaters of the river lie hundreds of miles upstream in the high plains of eastern New Mexico.

At the next fork, marked by a windmill and a sign, the trail turns left and away from the river. If you have time and energy, be sure to follow the route north along the Brazos as far as desired. The formal trail heads roughly straight west through open forest for the next mile. At about .25 mile along the way, a fork goes left, but continue straight west onto the section of trail not shown on the sign at the start of the hike. A faint road forks left after another .5 mile, but continue straight west. The trail finally turns south when it hits Big Creek.

The trail follows Big Creek to and across the paved park road. At the three-way junction across the road, go left into the forest. In less than .5 mile you return to the parking lot.

To extend the hike, combine it with parts of Hike 70. The trail is hot, humid, and buggy in the summer but pleasant the rest of the year. Be sure to walk the trails around some of the lakes to watch the alligators and birds during your visit. Give any alligators seen a wide berth; the park has safety guidelines for observing them. The park has an excellent developed campground; primitive camping isn't allowed. I did this hike on a beautiful spring weekend and, surprisingly, saw almost no one, although the bike trails around the lakes were crowded.

HIKE 70: *HALE LAKE*

General description: An easy day hike to a lake formed by a cut-off meander
General location: About forty-five miles southwest of Houston
Length: About 3.5 miles round trip
Elevation: 45-65 feet
Maps: Brazos Bend State Park map, Otey and Thompsons 7.5-minute USGS quads
Best season: Fall through spring
Water availability: Picnic area at Hale Lake
Special attractions: Lush forest, oxbow lake
Finding the trailhead: Follow the same directions as those for Hike 69, Brazos River, to Brazos Bend State Park. Drive into the park on the main road 3.2 miles to the Creekfield Lake Nature Trail parking area on the left.

The hike: Because of its proximity to Houston, Brazos Bend State Park is one of the most popular parks in the state. Many of its trails are used by both hikers and cyclists. This hike shares part of its route with bicycles. Short trails criss-cross the lush park, making many different routes possible.

The trail starts by following the Creekfield Lake Nature Trail across the road from the parking lot. The trail makes a big loop through dense woods around marshy Creekfield Lake before hitting the astronomical observatory. The new George Observatory isn't shown yet on most maps. Go left on the paved observatory trail about 100 feet back toward the lake, then turn right again back onto a dirt trail.

At about .25 mile past the observatory, the trail meets another trail. Go right on the new trail, crossing a board road that leads back to the observatory to the right. At about one mile, the trail crosses Big Creek on a combination road and foot bridge. Go right at the fork just across the bridge, toward Hale Lake.

The next fork lies at one end of horseshoe-shaped Hale Lake, formed when an old meander of Big Creek was cut off. Go right, to circle the lake in a counter-clockwise direction. The next fork on the left just goes out onto the point of land encircled by the curve of the lake. It makes a nice side trip through oaks cloaked in Spanish moss.

As you circle the lake, you will pass a picnic area on the right with water and bathrooms. Continue circling the lake until you return to the point where you first hit it near Big Creek. Go right and return to the trailhead by the same route. The hike can easily be extended by combinations with the trails used in Hike 69, Brazos River, or other trails.

If it's warm, you should see alligators sunning on some of the park's lakeshores. Maintain a respectful distance from any that you see. Follow the park safety guidelines with the alligators. No backcountry camping is allowed, but the park has an attractive developed campground. The park is usually hot, humid, and insect-infested in summer, but great the rest of the year.

HIKE 71: *WOODLANDS TRAIL*

General description: An easy day hike through the Big Thicket woods
General location: About fifteen miles east of Livingston
Length: About 5.4 miles round trip
Elevation: 195-270 feet
Maps: Big Thicket National Preserve Woodlands Trail brochure, Dallardsville 7.5-minute USGS quad
Best season: Fall through spring
Water availability: Big Sandy Creek
Special attractions: A fairly hilly part of the Big Thicket, pond
Finding the trailhead: From the US 190/US 59 intersection on the west side of Livingston, go east on US 190 about 13.3 miles to FM 1276 on the right. Follow FM 1276 about 3.4 miles to the parking area on the left side of the road marked with a "Big Sandy Creek Unit Parking" sign.

The hike: This hike lies in the most northwesterly unit of Big Thicket National Preserve. Of the original three million acres of the Big Thicket, maybe only 100,000 acres remain. The preserve protects 84,550 acres of this remnant. Most of the thicket lies on very low lying, relatively flat ground. The Big Sandy Creek Unit actually lies far enough north to have a few gentle hills.

The well-maintained trail is easy to follow. This hike follow the longer outer loop, but two shorter loops are possible. The trail forks right at the start. Take the short left fork for a view of the tranquil pond. The main trail follows the right fork. The trail starts in an old pine plantation and then crosses some open fields before entering the mixed pine and hardwood forest of the old thicket. The Park Service has placed wood posts marked with letters of the alphabet at each intersection and keyed them to the intersections on the map. They will help you find your way around the various loops.

I followed the loop in a counter-clockwise pattern. The east side of the loop follows along the floodplain by the creek. The trail climbs noticeably as it leaves the floodplain on the far side of the loop. Large loblolly pines, beeches, and

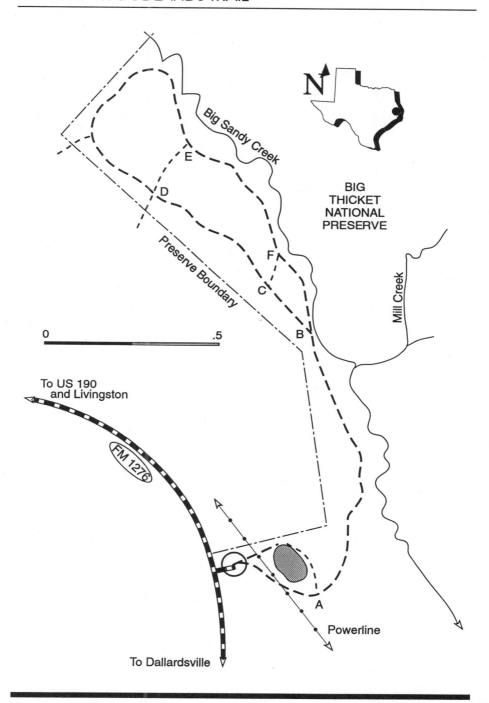

A tranquil pond lies at the start of the Woodlands Trail in the Big Thicket.

magnolias shade the upland part of the trail.

The path has many wooden footbridges, but you may still find some standing water on the trail. The footbridges are very slippery when wet. I found that the wettest part of the trail was in the first mile on my trip. If the creek is flooding, part of the trail will probably be underwater and unsafe to hike. As with all East Texas trails, this one is much more pleasant in the cooler months. Be sure to watch for poison ivy and carry insect repellent. Water can be taken from the creek if it is well purified. However, on this short a hike I recommend that you bring your own water.

HIKE 72: *BEECH WOODS*

General description: An easy day hike through mature beech-magnolia-loblolly forest

General location: Big Thicket National Preserve

Length: About six miles round trip

Elevation: 160-195 feet

Maps: Beech Woods Trail brochure (National Park Service), Spurger 7.5-minute USGS quad

Best season: Fall through spring

Water availability: Beech Creek

Special attractions: Mature Big Thicket forest

Permit: Required for camping

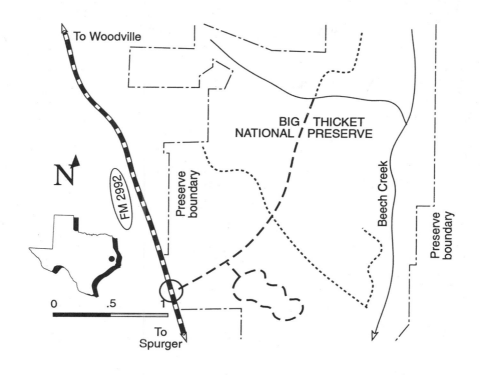

Finding the trailhead: Go about eight miles east of Woodville on FM 1746 and turn right on FM 2992. Go about 5.3 miles to the marked trailhead on the left.

The hike: Part of this hike wanders through a mature beech-magnolia-loblolly forest. The beech forest is one of several plant communities found in the lush Big Thicket of East Texas. Slight differences in slope, creek proximity, and soil create several different biological communities. The thicket forms a sort of crossroads between east and west. Prickly pears grow within a hundred yards of bald cypresses; roadrunners nest by eastern bluebirds.

The trail follows an old dirt road about .3 mile to the marked Beech Woods loop on the right. The loop wanders through beech forest. Unlike much of the thicket, the forest floor is open, with the canopy far above. Heavy logging, continuing to this day in most of East Texas, has cleared virtually all of the primeval forest. Much of it has been replanted in pine plantations. The national preserve was formed to protect a few representative tracts of the original three million acres plus covered by the Big Thicket.

After completing the loop, turn right and continue north on the dirt road. The road passes into dense second growth forest of pines, briars, and other plants.

After a little less than one mile, the trail hits a four-way junction. Feel free to explore the right and left forks, then continue straight ahead to Beech Creek at about 3.5 miles. The trail can be followed some distance further north if desired. Return via the same route. Backcountry camping is sometimes allowed on the northern part of this trail. A permit must be obtained at preserve headquarters.

Summers are usually hot, humid, and thick with mosquitoes and other insects, so the rest of the year is usually a better time for this hike. Carry raingear and insect repellant any time of year. Water can usually be obtained and purified from Beech Creek, but I recommend carrying your own.

HIKE 73: *SUNDEW TRAIL*

General description: A very easy day hike through pine-savannah wetlands
General location: Big Thicket National Preserve
Length: About one mile round trip
Elevation: 115-130 feet
Maps: Sundew Trail booklet (National Park Service), Warren 7.5-minute USGS quad
Best season: Fall through spring
Water availability: None
Special attractions: Carnivorous plants

HIKE 73 *SUNDEW TRAIL*

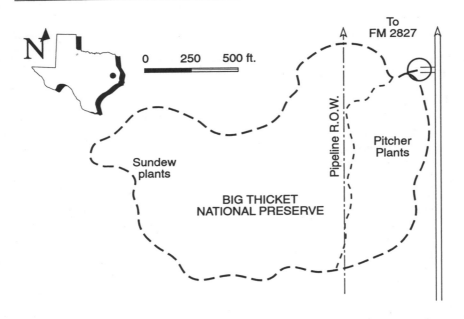

Finding the trailhead: Drive about seventeen miles south of Woodville on US 69-287 to FM 2827. Turn right and drive about .6 mile to a good dirt road on the left marked with a Big Thicket Sundew Trail sign. Drive about .5 mile down the dirt road to the marked parking area on the right.

The hike: The Sundew Trail lies in the Hickory Creek Savannah Unit of the Big Thicket National Preserve. The unit protects one of several biological associations found in the thicket. The short loop trail passes through acid bogs and a young stand of longleaf pines. Most of the plant community is fairly open, without the heavy forest common to much of the thicket. The extra sunlight makes the area better than average for producing wildflowers.

The hike follows a short, easy loop with boardwalks crossing the boggy areas. A shorter .25-mile loop is paved and wheelchair accessible. The young longleaf

Carnivorous pitcher plants eat insects to supplement the poor soils in which they grow.

pines found on part of the hike used to be common over much of southEast Texas. Unfortunately, they produce a very durable pine lumber and have been heavily logged. Since they are slow growing, loblolly and shortleaf pines are usually planted to replace them. The trees once grew to 125 feet tall, but very few old ones are left.

Be sure to look carefully for the two carnivorous plants, the pitcher plant and the sundew. Because of poor soils in their chosen habitat, they supplement their diet by trapping and consuming insects. Be sure to pick up the brochure and map at the trailhead; it will help you find the unique plants.

Since the trail is short, it can be done any time of year, but, as with other Big Thicket trails, the most comfortable hiking is in the fall through the spring.

HIKE 74: *KIRBY TRAIL*

General description: An easy day hike to Village Creek
General location: Big Thicket National Preserve
Length: About 2.4 miles round trip
Elevation: 100-50 feet
Maps: Kirby Nature Trail booklet, Kountze North 7.5-minute USGS quad
Best season: Fall through spring
Water availability: Trailhead
Special attractions: Large cypresses, lush forest
Finding the trailhead: Drive south of Woodville on US 69-287 about 24.5 miles (or about seven miles north of Kountze) to FM 420. Turn left, or east, and follow the signs about 2.7 miles to the Big Thicket Visitor Information Station on the left.

The hike: The Kirby Trail passes through several of the plant communities found in the Big Thicket. Numbered stops along the trail follow the interpretive guidebook available at the trailhead. This hike follows the outer loop, although shorter loops are possible. The preserve's temporary visitor information center is at the trailhead, along with chemical toilets.

Go left at the start of the loop at the trailhead. The trail descends through the slope forest community, dominated by beech, magnolia, and loblolly pine. The first two bridges cross very wet baygalls. The acidic water pooled in baygalls turns almost black from tannin leached from leaves. At about .7 mile, the trail forks. Unless it's flooded, be sure to go left onto the cypress loop. The trail passes some very large bald cypresses that somehow escaped loggers in earlier years. After about .3 mile the trail rejoins the other fork.

The trail follows floodplain forest above Village Creek and soon forks again. The numbered nature trail follows the shorter right fork; however, go left on the longer outer loop. A large new steel foot bridge crosses Village Creek just past the junction. By the time this book is printed, the trail on the other side of the bridge should be completed. It will connect with the Turkey Creek Trail (See Hike 75), making long hikes or backpacks possible.

After passing the bridge, the trail winds for about a mile and then rejoins the nature trail. Go left at the nature trail junction. The trail climbs back up into slope forest before ending the loop at the trailhead.

Be sure to take insect repellent on this hike. Poison ivy is common, especially on the forest floor in the floodplain area. Summers are hot and humid and have the most insects. If you have an extra day or two, rent a canoe in Kountze and paddle down a stretch of Village Creek, one of the classic Texas floats.

HIKE 74 *KIRBY TRAIL*

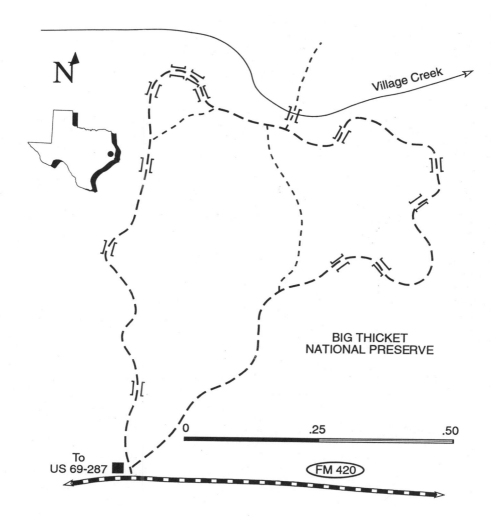

HIKE 75: *TURKEY CREEK*

General description: A moderate overnight hike along a winding Big Thicket Creek

General location: Big Thicket National Preserve

Length: About 18.4 miles round trip

Elevation: 140-75 feet

Maps: Turkey Creek Trail map (National Park Service), Hicksbaugh 7.5-minute USGS quad

Best season: Fall through spring

Water availability: Turkey Creek

Special attractions: Cypress sloughs, lush forest

Permit: Required for camping

Finding the trailhead: From Woodville, drive about thirteen miles south to Warren on US 69-287. Turn left, east, on FM 1943 and drive about four miles to the marked Turkey Creek trailhead and parking area on the right.

The hike: The Turkey Creek Trail is one of the longest and wildest trails in East Texas. It follows a creek that winds through one of several Big Thicket National Preserve units. Most of the original thicket is gone, lost to urban development, logging, agriculture, and oil and gas operations. This trail traverses one of the longest remaining relatively undisturbed parts of the original Big Thicket.

Don't let the trail length scare you. An easy car shuttle will halve the distance, and several intermediate trailheads make several even shorter hikes possible.

Very slight changes in elevation and soil create different environments along the trail route. Upland areas often have pine and oak forest, while creekside locations have cypresses and tupelos. The trail starts in an old pine plantation on relatively high ground but slowly drops down closer to the creek. Wooden mile markers will help you pace yourself as you follow the trail. Boardwalks and bridges cross most of the wet areas. Benches have been at built at periodic intervals, nice considering all the wetness and mud during some parts of the year.

Just past two miles, the trail merges with an abandoned dirt road. Turn right onto the road for a short distance; then turn left back onto the trail. At almost three miles, the trail forks. If you have time, be sure to go left a quarter mile on the Pitcher Plant Trail to see the carnivorous plants. The Pitcher Plant Trail also makes a good alternate trailhead for a shorter hike or car shuttle. Turn right, following the Turkey Creek signs at the junction, to continue the main hike.

After the junction, the trail turns toward the creek and enters the floodplain. Huge oaks and other trees create a dense forest canopy. Near the creek, at about four miles, large bald cypresses become common and line the sloughs. At the six-mile bench, great for a breather, the trail follows a bluff relatively high above the creek. Just past it, the trail hits a dirt county road (another possible trailhead). Turn right on the road and cross Turkey Creek on the road bridge. Just past the bridge, turn left and follow the signs back into the forest on the trail.

At about 6.5 miles, the trail passes through some very large old pines. Just before the nine-mile point, the trail crosses a swampy baygall on the longest and last boardwalk (bridge 29, no less!). The trail ends at a paved county road a short distance further.

By the time this book is printed, the Park Service should have completed a six-mile extension of this trail. The trail will continue along Turkey Creek from the ending trailhead above to the Kirby Trail (See Hike 74).

Be sure to take insect repellent on this hike, especially in late spring and summer. Considering the lowland nature of this hike, it's very well designed. I hiked the full length in a very wet spring and only had trouble with water in a few places. The hike will be very hot and humid in summer. Poison ivy is common on the forest floor. Purify any water taken from the creek.

Spring is the wettest time of year and the most likely time for the trail to be flooded. If the creek is out of its banks at the road bridges at the north and south trailheads, the trail will probably be under water. Don't attempt to follow the trail through flooded areas; it's too easy to get lost or fall into a deep hole.

Massive bald cypresses thrive in sloughs in the Big Thicket.

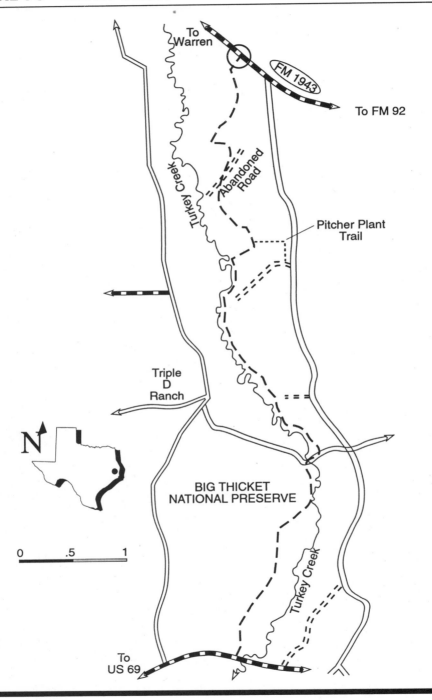

ADDITIONAL INFORMATION

Federal agencies

Angelina National Forest
1907 Atkinson Dr.
P.O. Box 756
Lufkin, TX 75901
(409) 639-8620

Aransas National Wildlife Refuge
P.O. Box 100
Austwell, TX 77950
(512) 286-3559

Army Corps of Engineers
  (Grapevine Lake)
110 Fairway Drive
Grapevine, TX 76051
(817) 481-4541

Army Corps of Engineers
  (Lake Texoma)
Denison Dam
Rt. 4, Box 493
Denison, TX 75020
(903) 465-4990

Big Bend National Park
Big Bend National Park
TX 79834
(915) 477-2251

Big Thicket National Preserve
3785 Milam
Beaumont, TX 77701
(409) 839-2689

Davy Crockett National Forest
1240 E. Loop 304
Crockett, TX 75835
(409) 544-2046

Fort Davis National Historic Site
P.O. Box 1456
Fort Davis, TX 79734
(915) 426-3224

Guadalupe Mountains
  National Park
HC 60, Box 400
Salt Flat, TX 79847
(915) 828-3251

Laguna Atascosa National
  Wildlife Refuge
Box 450
Rio Hondo, TX 78583
(210) 748-3607

Padre Island National Seashore
9405 South Padre Island Drive
Corpus Christi, TX 78418
(512) 937-2621

Sam Houston National Forest
Raven District
P.O. Drawer 1000
New Waverly, TX 77358
(409) 344-6205

Sam Houston National Forest
San Jacinto District
308 N. Belcher
Cleveland, TX 77327
(713) 592-6461

Santa Ana National
  Wildlife Refuge
Rt. 2, Box 202A
Alamo, TX 78516
(210) 787-3079

State agencies

Texas Parks and Wildlife
  Department (headquarters)
4200 Smith School Road
Austin, TX 78744 (512) 389-4890

Bastrop State Park
Box 518
Bastrop, TX 78602
(512) 321-2101

Bentsen-Rio Grande State Park
P.O. Box 988
Mission, TX 78572
(210) 585-1107

Big Bend Ranch State Natural Area
HCR 70, Box 375
Terlingua, TX 79853
(915) 424-3327

Brazos Bend State Park
21901 FM 762
Needville, TX 77461
(409) 553-3243

Buescher State Park
P.O. Box 75
Smithville, TX 78957
(512) 237-2241

Caddo Lake State Park
Route 2, Box 15
Karnack, TX 75661
(903) 679-3351

Caprock Canyons State Park
P.O. Box 204
Quitaque, TX 79255
(806) 455-1492

Colorado Bend State Park
Box 118
Bend, TX 76824
(915) 628-3240

Daingerfield State Park
Route 1, Box 286-B
Daingerfield, TX 75638
(903) 645-2921

Davis Mountains State Park
Box 786
Fort Davis, TX 79734
(915) 426-3337

Dinosaur Valley State Park
Box 396
Glen Rose, TX 76043
(817) 897-4588

Eisenhower State Park
Route 2, Box 50K
Denison, TX 75020
(903) 465-1956

Enchanted Rock State Natural Area
Route 4, Box 170
Fredericksburg, TX 78624
(915) 247-3903

Fairfield Lake State Park
Route 2, Box 912
Fairfield, TX 75840
(903) 389-4514

Franklin Mountains State Park
P.O. Box 200
Canutillo, TX 79835-9998
(915) 877-1528

Hueco Tanks State Park
Rural Route 3, Box 1
El Paso, TX 79935
(915) 857-1135

Huntsville State Park
P.O. Box 508
Huntsville, TX 77340
(409) 295-5644

State agencies *(continued)*

Inks Lake State Park
Route 2, Box 31
Burnet, TX 78611
(512) 793-2223

Lake Livingston State Park
Route 9, Box 1300
Livingston, TX 77351
(409) 365-2201

Lake Mineral Wells State Park
Route 4, Box 39C
Mineral Wells, TX 76067
(817) 328-1171

Lake Somerville State
  Park (Birch Creek)
Route 1, Box 499
Somerville, TX 77879
(409) 535-7763

Lake Somerville State
  Park (Nails Creek)
Route 1, Box 61C
Ledbetter, TX 78946
(409) 289-2392

Lost Maples State Natural Area
HC01, Box 156
Vanderpool, TX 78885
(210) 966-3413

Matagorda Island State Park
P.O. Box 117
Port O'Connor, TX 77982-0117
(512) 983-2215

Meridian State Park
Box 188
Meridian, TX 76665
(817) 435-2536

Monahans Sandhills State Park
Box 1738
Monahans, TX 79756
(915) 943-2092

Palmetto State Park
Route 5, Box 201
Gonzales, TX 78629
(210) 672-3266

Palo Duro Canyon State Park
Route 2, Box 285
Canyon, TX 79015
(806) 488-2227

Pedernales Falls State Park
Route 1, Box 450
Johnson City, TX 78636
(512) 868-7304

Seminole Canyon State Park
P.O. Box 820
Comstock, TX 78837
(915) 292-4464

Other agencies

Austin Parks and
  Recreation Department
1500 W. Riverside Drive
Austin, TX 78704
(512) 499-6700

Cibolo Wilderness Trail
Box 9
Boerne, TX 78006
(512) 537-4141

Houston Arboretum and
  Nature Center
4501 Woodway Drive
Houston, TX 77024
(713) 681-8433

Parks Information
Travis County PITD
P.O. Box 1748
Austin, TX 78767
(512) 264-2740 or 472-7483

Trinity Trail: Open Space Program
Collin County Public Works
210 S. McDonald Street
McKinney, TX 75069
(214) 548-4619

ADDITIONAL READING

Evans, Harry. 50 Hikes in Texas. Gem Guides Book Co., Pico Rivera, CA, Third Edition 1983.

Ganci, Dave. Hiking the Southwest: Arizona, New Mexico, and West Texas. Sierra Club Books, San Francisco, CA, 1983.

Hiker's Guide to Trails of Big Bend National Park. Big Bend Natural History Association, Big Bend National Park, TX, 1978.

Little, Mickey. Hiking and Backpacking Trails of Texas. Gulf Publishing, Houston, TX, Third Edition 1990.

Miller, George Oxford and Delena Tull. Texas Parks and Campgrounds. Gulf Publishing, Houston, TX, Second Edition 1990.

ABOUT THE AUTHOR

Patricia and Laurence Parent

Laurence Parent was born and raised in New Mexico. After receiving an engineering degree at the University of Texas at Austin, he practiced engineering for six years before becoming a full-time freelance photographer and writer specializing in landscape, travel, and nature subjects. His photos appear in Sierra Club, Audubon, and many other calendars. His article and photo credits include *National Geographic Traveler, Outside, Backpacker, Sierra,* and the *New York Times.* He contributes regularly to regional publications such as *Texas Highways, Texas Monthly, New Mexico Magazine,* and *Texas Parks & Wildlife.* Other work includes posters, advertising, museum exhibits, postcards, and brochures.

He has completed several books, including one for Falcon Press, "The Hiker's Guide to New Mexico." His work also appears in Falcon's "New Mexico on My Mind" and "Texas on My Mind" books, Falcon Press calendars, and other Falcon products. He makes his home in Austin, Texas with his wife Patricia.

HIKING NOTES

HIKING NOTES

HIKING NOTES

HIKING NOTES

HIKING NOTES